THE internal character of a man is often expressed in his exterior appearance, even in the manner of his walking and in the sound of his voice. Likewise the hidden character of things is to a certain extent expressed in their outward forms . . . He ought to look with his own eyes into the book of Nature and become able to understand it . . . The knowledge of nature as it is—not as we imagine it to be—constitutes true philosophy . . . But he who is not true himself will not see the truth as it is taught by nature, and it is far easier to study a number of books and to learn by heart a number of scientific theories than to ennoble one's own character to such an extent as to enter into perfect harmony with nature and to be able to see the truth . . . Wisdom in man is nobody's servant and has not lost its own freedom, and through wisdom man attains power over the stars . . . He must realize the presence of the highest in his own heart before he can know it with his intellect. The spiritual temple is locked with many keys, and those who are vain enough to believe that they can invade it by their own power, and without being shown the way by the light of wisdom, will storm against it in vain. Wisdom is not created by man; it must come to him, and cannot be purchased for money nor coaxed with promises, but it comes to those whose minds are pure and whose hearts are open to receive it . . . The highest a man can feel and think is his highest ideal, and the higher we rise in the scale of existence and the more our knowledge expands, the higher will be our ideal. As long as we cling to our highest ideal we will be happy in spite of the sufferings and vicissitudes of life. The highest ideal confers the highest and most enduring happiness . . . The highest power of the intellect, if it is not illuminated by love, is only a high grade of animal intellect, and will perish in time; but the intellect animated by the love of the Supreme is the intellect of the angels, and will live in eternity. All things are vehicles of virtues, everything in nature is a house wherein dwell certain powers and virtues such as God has infused throughout Nature and which inhabit all things in the same sense as the soul is in man . . . True faith is spiritual consciousness, but a belief based upon mere opinions and creeds is the product of ignorance, and is superstition . . . This physical body, which is believed to be of so little importance by those who love to dream about the mysteries of the spirit, is the most secret and valuable thing. It is the true "stone which the builders rejected," but which must become the corner-stone of the temple. It is the "stone" which is considered worthless by those who seek for a God above the clouds and reject Him when He enters their house. This physical body is not merely an instrument for divine power, but it is also the soil from which that which is immortal in man receives its strength.

—PARACELSUS

FRANK LLOYD WRIGHT

THE LIVING CITY

HORIZON PRESS NEW YORK 1958

711.4
W

A portion of this work was published under the
title *When Democracy Builds,* copyright 1945.

CONTENTS

6

LIST OF ILLUSTRATIONS

FOREWORD

WHEN a great Oak is to die, a few yellow-green leaves appear on topmost branches. Next season much of the upper part of the tree is yellow; next year the upper branches remain without leaves. After several following seasons we say the tree is "dry."

But for many years to come, the frame of the dry tree stands erect, making black marks against the sky as though nothing had happened. Finally, rotted at the root, useless, the top-heavy structure falls. But then even the heavy frame must lie a long time broken upon the ground. Many years pass before it crumbles to soil and grass roots come; perhaps another acorn or two to give rise to other great oaks.

What sap and leaves were to the great Oak a healthy aesthetic is to a People.

This book is written in firm belief that true human culture has a healthy sense of the beautiful as its life-of-the-soul: an aesthetic organic, as *of* life itself, not *on* it; nobly relating man to his environment. The sense of this natural aesthetic would make of man a gracious, integral, potent part of the whole of human life. Ethics, Art and Religion survive in civilizations only as departments of this aesthetic sense, and survive only to the extent that they embody human sentiment for the beautiful. To ignore this truth is to misunderstand the soul of man, to turn him over to science ignorant of his true significance; and to remain blind to his destiny.

Here we are in this great melting-pot of all the breaking-down or cast-off cultures of a world wherein we have allowed the present arrogance of science to forestall a genuine culture of our own. In common we inherit and are preserving this cultural lag.

To confess that we "the great American people" have, as yet, developed no culture of our own, no efflorescence of the great Tree of Life, no such fragrance, is quite fair enough. Useful at this time.

Just as great trees die, civilizations themselves die—often withered from within by lack of culture. Or they are blown down, destroyed root and branch by the eradicable pest—war. Or are buried by the flood—revolution.

We are too young a nation thus to degenerate? Too vigorous to die a violent death utterly?

Although we have never attained the high plane from which a nation degenerates, the virus of earlier cultures coming here in the blood of immigrants might be a contagion marking us for decay and death.

Salvation depends upon the realization that, with science carried far enough and deep enough, we will find great art to be the sure significance of all that science can ever know of life and see that art and religion are valid prophecy of everything science may ever live to convey. We will find philosophy to be the science of man from *within* the man himself. Our vaunted scientists must work upon him only from the *outside,* so where man's soul is concerned science must work in vain; because such sciences as we practice substitute morality for ethics, money for ideas, fact for truth. We, as a nation, have ignored or only imitated art, confused or neglected religion, demoralized philosophy and ignored ethics. No science can be humanely fruitful until art, religion, philosophy, ethics and science are comprehended as one great entity, a universal Unity seen as the Beautiful.

In this immense drift of provincial conformity-culture, our aesthetic sense is neglected, or betrayed, and likely to come down to a raising of the overflowing cup with the little finger delicately lifted: discussing, say, the easel-picture directed to the nervous system instead of the soul. Or some poetic pose or selecticism by taste; taste in manners or the cliché all over again in Architecture. Whereas we need now to know that the honest hardships of our forefathers in their bravest pioneering were as nothing compared to the equivocal trials now inflicted upon their sons and daughters on this new frontier of the Spirit: in behalf of a culture of our own! Not

10

only we, their sons and daughters, but our grandsons and granddaughters must stand here now exposed to insidious danger from decaying traditions within and blind authority without.

Our forefathers faced dangers in the open that we might live. We face more insidious dangers: the danger of degeneracy, of dishonesty; the danger that they may have lived for us in vain and we, their own begotten sons and daughters, will have begotten sons and daughters of our own in vanity without the heritage of spiritual courage and consequent strength.

"Once upon a time," not so long ago, the conquering of physical or territorial realm was the Frontier. But now to conquer sordid, ugly commercialism in this machine age, this "bony fiber of the dry tree"—that spiritual conquest is our new Frontier. Only by growing a healthy aesthetic, organic in the souls of our young polyglot nationals can we win this victory, greatest of all victories—Democracy.

This book is on the firing line of this new, most important frontier of all frontiers—a fight for faith, faith in man's Democracy, in the beauty of this new gospel of individuality; faith in the beauty that is the fragrant efflorescence of all humanity—the sap and foliage of the Living Tree—man's faith in himself as Himself.

—F. Ll. W.

NOTE

PROFESSIONAL criticism (say, writing book reviews) like most criticism, requires extreme egotism. But critics are not so useless as they might seem to be.

Among apprehensive appreciations of the original *When Democracy Builds* (reviews by critics more interested in content than style) came several more interested in style than content.

One such said, "The style of the work is just this side of deplorable," and quoted a sentence to prove it. I have retained this sentence. Another said, "The licentious use of capitals is confusing." So it seemed. Even to me.

One poor man gave it up entirely, saying he "failed to understand."

Another said the book was full of clichés. Yes, it was; but "my own"— because quoting myself.

So, curiosity thus aroused many months away from initial writing, I took up the book to reread it. Perspective was afforded by distance from the act—and—

Well . . . the critics were all too kind. The style of the work seemed to me —yes—deplorable. Capitalization by means of which I intended to emphasize significances actually confused them. Sentences pregnant to me with meaning when I wrote them utterly failed to clinch, or went into reverse.

What to do?

Rewrite the book.

Ignominy of course!

I hardened into my own most severe critic, I thought, and yet—sentences quoted by my critics to show my style just this side of "deplorable" I found right enough—in their way. They stand. I apologize. But I did find the affair with capitalization fantastic, far too capitalistic. I threw this affair out, and proceeded to clinch every phrase in the book concerned with an idea, so far as I could. I found so very many at loose ends and many stay there yet.

But as for clichés, if so, I made the original of every cliché *myself*. Regarding that I call your attention to the captious English lady who, advised to read *Hamlet*, threw the book away half-read—with the contemptuous remark that she "couldn't see why they thought Shakespeare so great an author when his work was so full of quotations."

My critics! Sincerely I thank you.

—F. Ll. W.

TALIESIN

14

PART ONE

NATURE

Earth

THE value of Earth as man's heritage, or of Man as earth's great heritage, is gone far from him now in any big city centralization has built (but never designed). Centralization—without plan—has overbuilt. Urban happiness of the properly citified citizen consists in crowding in confusion —lured by the hypnotic warmth, pressure and approbation of the crowd? The screech and mechanical uproar of the big city turns the citified head, fills citified ears—as the song of birds, wind in the trees, animal cries, or as the voices and songs of his loved ones once filled his heart. He is sidewalk-happy.

But where and as he now stands, out of the machine that his big city of the motor age has become, no citizen creates or operates more than mere machinery nor is he going to be much more than a machine himself—if his big city stays.

Thus the properly citified citizen becomes a broker of profit-system ideas, a vendor of gadgetry, a salesman dealing for profit in human exaggeration. A speculator in frailties continually dealing in the ideas and inventions of others—or become an avid spectator. This puller of levers, pusher of the buttons of vicarious power, has power of his own only by way of mechanical craft. A "graft" is this tide on which he rides.

So a parasite of the spirit is here; dervish in a whirling vortex. Yes—from the top down, and enamored of the whirl.

Perpetual to-and-fro excites this citified citizen, robs him of deeper sympathy, of the meditation and reflection once his as he lived and walked under clean sky among the fresh greenery to which he was born companion. On solid earth he was neither fool-proof nor weather-proof, but he was a whole man.

But he has traded his Book of Creation for emasculation by way of the convenient substitute; traded his origins and native pastimes with streams, woods, fields, and animals for the ubiquitous, habitual to-and-fro; taint of carbon monoxide rising from him to his rented aggregations of hard cells on upended streets overlooking hard pavements. "Paramounts," "Roxies," night clubs, bars—such as these are his relaxation, his urban recourse. For all this easy come and easy go he lives in some cubicle among other cubicles under a landlord himself a "hot-shot"—one who probably lives up there above him in a "penthouse." Both landlord and tenant are the living apotheosis of rent. Rent! Always rent in some form is the city. If not quite yet parasites—parisitic all.

So exists the properly citified urbanite! Still a slave to the herd-instinct, fatally committed to vicarious power—a *slave* in any final analysis just as the medieval laborer, not so long before him, was slave to caprice of king or state. A cultural weed now, he grows rank in the urban field.

This weed goes to seed! Children keep on coming and growing. Now herded by the thousand in schools built like factories, run like factories: all systematically turning out herd-struck teenagers like machines turning out shoes. In knowledge-factories.

And when urban men-of-commerce themselves succeed, they become more than ever vicarious? Soon these very successful men sink into the sham luxury their city life so continually produces. But they *create* nothing! Spiritually impotent, a fixation has them where impotence wants them: fixation in a cliché.

But life itself has become intolerably restless; a mere tenant of the big landlord: the "big city." Yes . . . above the belt, if he is properly citified, the citizen has long lost sight of the true aim of normal human existence. He has accepted not only substitute means but substitute aims and ends. Naturally gregarious himself, his life now tends toward the promiscuous, blind adventure of the crafty animal; toward some form of graft; toward the febrile pursuit of sex as "relief" from factual routine. He seeks but cannot

18

find peace in an all prevailing uproar of mechanical conflicts—unless in alcohol? Meantime struggling artificially to maintain teeth, hair, muscles, and sap; his sight growing dim; hearing increasingly by telephone. He now must go against or across a streaming tide of traffic, at risk of damage or death to himself or others. His own good time is inevitably, regularly, increasingly wasted by others because he is as determined, and inevitably, all-out to waste theirs. All go about in different directions or swarm over hard concrete to various ugly scaffoldings, or go underground to get into other cubicles occupied by other sub-parasites-of-rent—always rent, rent in some form—or go higher up under some other skyscraper-rentlord. The citizen's entire life is an *exaggeration* or frustration, on wheels or accelerated by plane, television or telephone. By elevator, the upended street, his life is thus limited and confused, contained instead of *expanded;* a vicarious life virtually sterilized by machinery, by medicine, by more and more stimulants. His demoralization has only begun.

Were motor oil and castor oil to dry up, the great big city would soon cease to function: the citizens would promptly perish.

So this modern monster, degeneration of the Renaissance city, becomes the form universal of anxiety, all stated in various form of rent. The citizen's very life is tenant, himself rented, in a rented world. He and his ever-growing family evicted if in arrears, or the vast "debt system" of rent goes to smash.

Should his nervous pace slacken, his digestion become ulcerous or fail, his anxious lock-step with rent would fall out with the lock-step of "production." Landlord, money-lord, and machine-lord . . . the man, with ulcers or none, is soon a total loss even to his bureaucratic government.

Nevertheless—relentlessly—over him, beside him and beneath him, even in his heart as he sleeps, is fear. Fear. Fear forever ticking in this taxi-meter of triple rent—rent for land, rent for money, rent for being alive—each of them goading the anxious "consumer's" unceasing struggle for or against ominous increase-of-production. Production regardless—production now driving consumption bankrupt or insane; insatiable unearned increment for power. To stay in the lock-step—that is now all the "pay-off" he hopes for. Not so much more than that. He, the wage-slave in some form, puts his own life into bondage, or is busy managing to get the lives of others there just in order to keep up the superficial privileges to which he has consciously, fatuously, subscribed and which are often described to him as great, beneficent "free enterprise": enterprise to which his ubiquitous politicians continually refer him. Humanity is here preying upon humanity? Man's inhumanity to man seems also to be the feature of the only "economic system" the urban citizen yet knows or has been, officially, encouraged by government to know. So he takes "the system" for granted—as now he takes all else for granted: Capitalism included. But even "the system" is, at best, only capitalistic. Not true capitalism because it is the apex instead of the base of the pyramid that is on the ground.

As the citizen stands, powerful modern resources, naturally his own by uses of modern machinery, are (owing to their very nature) turning against him, although the system he lives under is one he himself helped build. Such centralizations of men and capital as he must now serve are no longer wise or humane. Long ago—having done all it could do for humanity—the centralization we call the big city became a centripetal force grown beyond our control; agitated by rent to continually additional, vicarious powers.

Thus the system is steadily increasing in man his animal instincts, his fear of being turned out of the hole into which he has been accustomed to crawl in again each evening to crawl out again next morning. Natural horizontality—true line of human freedom on earth—is going, or gone. The citizen condemns himself to perhaps natural but most unbecoming (and now unprofitable to him) pig-piling. What he aspires to is a sterile urban verticality, actually unnatural to him because he is upended, suspended and traffic-jammed by this verticality due to his own mad excess. He is calling this evidence of fixability instead of flexibility—*success*. It is only conformity.

Notwithstanding slum-clearance by insurance, the profit-sharing of sporadic "housing" which he has unwittingly approved to build himself permanently into bondage, he becomes more confused and helpless.

Nevertheless out of this automatic turnabout against him of his own industrial revolution without a soul now fast running away from modern man, he may yet emerge from the ancient shadow-of-the-wall as master instead of machine-age conscript. He may emerge by way of Organic Architecture because its philosophy and practice are natural to his better self made free.

The Shadow-of-the-Wall—Primitive Instincts Still Alive

Go back far enough in time. Mankind was divided into cave-dwelling agrarians and wandering tribes of hunter-warriors; and we might find the wanderer swinging from branch to branch in the leafy bower of the tree, insured by the curl at the end of his tail, while the more stolid lover of the wall lurked, for safety, hidden in some hole in the ground or in a cave: the ape?

The static cave-dweller was ancient conservative. Probably he was more brutal, if not more ferocious, with his heavy club when occasion arose than the mobile wanderer with his slender spear.

The cave-dweller became cliff-dweller. He began to build cities. Establishment was his idea. His God was a malicious murderer. His own statue, made by himself more terrible than himself, was really his God; a God also hiding away. He erected this God into a mysterious covenant. When he could, he made his God of gold. He still does.

But his swifter, more mobile brother devised a more adaptable and elusive dwelling-place—the folding tent.

He, nomad, went in changing seasons from place to place, over the whole earth following the laws of change: natural to him.

He was the Adventurer.

His God was a Spirit: like a wind, devastating or beneficent as he was himself.

These main divisions of primitive man, the human family, having herd-instinct in common with other animals, made God, or conceived gods, in their own image. Both human divergencies set up enmity. Enmity each toward the other.

Cave-dwellers bred their young in the shadow of the wall. Mobile wanderers bred theirs under the stars in such safety as seclusion by distance from the enemy might afford.

21

We assume the cave-dweller multiplied with comparative ease owing to this safety, and more rapidly than his brother the wanderer. But when his defenses fell, destruction was more complete, economic waste more terrific. So when he ceased to find a natural cave, he learned to make one. As he grew more powerful, his walls grew heavier. Fortification became his own; cities were, originally, such fortifications. Early dwellings were only less so. He, the cave-dweller, was thus prototype of the state socialist, communist, or statist. Not the democrat.

The cave-dweller's nomadic human counterpart meantime cultivated mobility for safety. Defenses, for him, lay in the Idea—or swiftness, stratagem, and such arts of self-defense as nature taught.

These primitive instincts of the human race—now ingrown instead of outgrowing in this far distance of time—are still at work; although instincts of the wandering tribe seem to have been overcome gradually by the more material defenses and heavier static establishment of the original cave-dweller. Herein we still see the "shadow of this wall."

I imagine the ideal of freedom which keeps breaking through our present static establishments, setting their features aside, or obliterating them, is due in no small degree to survival of the original instincts of the nomad—the adventurer: he who kept his freedom by his undivided prowess beneath the stars rather than he who lived by his obedience and labor in the deep shadow of the wall.

The nomad? Is he thus prototype of the democrat?

However that may be, these conflicting human natures have conquered or been vanquished, married, intermarried, brought forth other natures; a fusion in some, still a straining confusion in others. In some men, a survival, more or less distinct, of one or the other of these salient, archaic instincts of mankind.

Gradually in the present body of mankind, both natural instincts work together and produce what we call civilization. All civilization insists upon and strives to perfect culture, in order that it may survive. By increasing happiness?

In the affair of culture, "shadow-of-the-wall" has so far seemed predominant, although the open sky of the adventurer appeals more and more today to the human spirit. As physical fear of brutal force grows less, all need of fortification grows less. Ingrained yearning of the mobile hunter for freedom now finds more truth and reason for being than the stolid masonry defenses (cave-dwelling) once upon a time erected in necessity to protect human life from humankind. This freedom is now characteristic of all yearning for culture—a spirit still slumbering in the agrarian and the manufacturer, the merchant and the artist.

Yes—modern science makes all ancient, static defenses useless. Man's value now depends not so much upon what he has made static (that is to say, saved, stored up, fortified) as upon what he can *do*—still better—by proper use of new scientific resources. So a human type is emerging capable of rapidly changing environment to fit desires, one amply able to offset the big city of today: remnant of the great, ancient "Wall." In this capability to change we have the new type of citizen. We call him democratic.

It is evident that modern life must be served more naturally and conserved by more space and light, by greater freedom of movement. And by more general expression of the individual in practice of the ideal we now call culture in civilization. A new space-concept is needed. It is becoming more evident everywhere. A definite phase of this new Ideal comes in what we call organic architecture—the *natural* architecture of the democratic spirit in this age of the machine.

Our modern automobility is only one of the leading factors of modernity. Alongside glass and steel it is having characteristic effect upon what survives of the nature of the cave-dweller. He places his faith with the new facilities, speed and command of time and distance, instead of in his own works. But these scientific future-liberating factors of the machine age are actually his means of potential self-realization. But the modern citizen will use them for more human freedom when he uses them at all well. Man is returning to the descendants of the wandering tribe—the adventurers, I hope.

The machine is continuously at work—molding, remodeling, relentlessly driving human character in many directions—mobile. The question is becoming more one of grass or goods? *Men* or *Man.*

23

So it has already come true in our overgrown cities of today that the terms of feudal thinking are changing, if not by name, to terms of money and commercial diplomacy. But the old form of city, except as a market, has little or nothing substantial to give modern civilization above wagery, little or nothing above the belt—except degeneration.

New York is the biggest mouth in the world. It appears to be prime example of the survival of the herd instinct, leading the universal urban conspiracy to beguile man from his birthright (the good ground), to hang him by his eyebrows from skyhooks above hard pavements, to crucify him, sell him, or be sold by him. He is now himself a form of rent called production for profit. High priests of such gangsteristics we have set up in politics or in professional armchairs. High priests of religion as of education, as we have them both now, seldom understand and never dare teach the basic freedom, the life-blood of Democracy, ethical and not militant! Its very nature remains obscure. Through new powers of publicity (the power of reiteration) mediocre high priests overtake and imprison a mediocre citizenry. Conformity to mediocrity increases. Into high places go common men. Enormous urban flocks meantime sing false hymns to vicarious power, jazzing a dreary dirge. These theme songs are as false to the singer as to the listener. All badly off key.

Ultimate impotence comes where creation of fine art is the concern. This price is extracted from us, as a nation, by the momentous mistake of substituting artificiality—artificial means of production and machine power —for human power, in terms of money.

Instead of expanding our spiritual strength as human beings by means of these our new scientific advantages, we are content to practice artifice without art. The Substitute or Imitation is the signpost of our cultural lag. Science can do little or nothing about all this. It is up to the American spirit seeking above things for organic (*natural*) forms truly essential to a culture of our own.

Democracy: Gospel of Individuality

Only human values are life-giving values.

No organic values are ever life-taking. When man builds "natural" buildings naturally, he builds his very life into them—inspired by intrinsic Nature in this interior sense we are here calling "organic." Instead the citizen is now trained to see life as a cliché whereas his architect should train his own mind, and thereby the citizen's, to see the nature of glass as Glass, the board as Board, a brick as Brick; see the nature of steel as Steel: see all in relation to each other as well as in relation to Time, Place, and Man. Be eager to be honest with himself and so not untrue to other men; desire deeply to live on harmonious terms with Man and Nature; try to live in the richer sense because deep *in* nature: be native as trees to the wood, as grass to the floor of the valley. Only then can the democratic spirit of man, individual, rise out of the confusion of communal life in the city to a creative civilization of the ground. We are calling that civilization of man and ground—really organic agronomy—democracy: intrinsically superior to the more static faiths of the past lying now in ruins all about him. If the Usonian citizen were to live in a free city of democracy he could not fail to make communal life richer for all the world because true individual independence—by natural growth of a natural conscience—would be his. The American citizen is now where he must abandon his favorite expedients—especially the idea that money plus authority can rule the world. He must at last realize that ideas inspired by spiritual integrity can and will make the modern world.

Faith in that conscientious selfhood is the ideal fit for the sons of the sons of American Democracy.

What then is the Nature of this idea we call organic architecture? We are here calling this architecture The Architecture of Democracy. Why?

Because it is intrinsically based on Nature-law: law *for* man not law *over* man. So understood, so applied. It is simply the human spirit given appropriate architectural form. Simply, too, it is the material structure of every man's life on earth now seen by him as various forms of structure—in short, organic. Democracy possesses the material means today to be enlarged intelligently and turned about now to employ machine power on super-materials for man's own superiority. Therefore, organic architecture is not satisfied to be employed merely to make money—not if that money is to be stacked against Man himself. Our growing dissatisfaction with auto-cratic power or bureaucracy of any kind requires wisdom. Old wisdom and good sense are modern even now; it is their application that changes.

Still more ancient is the wisdom, and it too is modern, that recognizes this new democratic concept of man free in a life wherein money and land-laws are established as subordinate to rights of the human being. That means first of all that good architecture is good democracy.

So dignity and worth would come to our society if the individual were thus *individual;* true individuality, no longer written off as some kind of personal idiosyncracy by way of "taste" but protected as essence, to be understood as the safest basis for interpretation of science, the practice of art, ultimately the inspiration of a true religion. This is modern today; it always was; it always will be. Now in order to become *organic* we will learn to *understand* that form and function are as *one.* On that organic basis a civilization might endure forever as a happy humane circumstance. Free.

This new sense-of-the-within naturally unfolding, taking form by the culture of art, architecture, philosophy and religion, natural; all being con-tent to look *within* to the Spirit for the solution of every human problem and, by expanding the means so found, enlarging and achieving new, varied expressions of life on earth—this would be old wisdom, ancient as Laotze at least; yet modern. That is modern Architecture and modern manhood.

Were we in America to put this concept to work in government, that would be our great day-after-tomorrow? If it were basic in what is now carelessly miscalled "education" we would soon arrive at proper qualifica-tion of the vote. And we would arrive at the sense-of-the-within as the new criterion in art and architecture. By means of it, architecture will be able to qualify the work of the world, reject the imitation and the substitute; make any makeshift a stupidity or a crime. Make life one great integral sim-plicity: Beauty comes alive.

Such simplicity is necessarily not "plainness." A barn door is not simple; it is merely plain, sterile. Harmonious grace of the wild flower and all countenances of organic integrity anywhere or everywhere are truly simple. In all man-made life-concerns this is integral Simplicity. If organic, simplicity is in itself exuberant. It was ever modern in ancient times. Why not so now?

This our integrity needs—old wisdom, yet new to our present servile, provincial, and amazing civilization. Infinite possibilities exist to make of the city a place suitable for the free man in which freedom can thrive and the soul of man grow, a City of cities that democracy could approve and so desperately needs; will soon demand? Yes, and in that vision of decentralization and reintegration lies our natural twentieth century dawn. Of such is the nature of the democracy free men may honestly call the new freedom. Where and whenever this is understood, the part is to the whole no less than the whole is to the part. This true entity is alone able to live as organic architecture or as culture—the soul of any civilization.

PART TWO

FAIRCHILD AERIAL SURVEYS, INC. N.Y.

FIND THE CITIZEN

ILLUSION

Social and Economic Disease

TO look at the cross section of any plan of a big city is to look at something like the section of a fibrous tumor. In the light of the space-needs of the twentieth century we see there not only similar inflamed exaggerations of tissue but more and more painfully forced circulation; comparable to high blood pressure in the human system. Think of the big towns you know; then try to imagine what modern mobility and new space-annihilating facilities, even now, are doing to them! Consider the space-requirement of modern mobilized man today as compared with twenty years ago. At least twenty times larger?

Growing out of the old feudal city-plan are these new *centripetal* centralizations: unrecognized uneconomic forces at work to destroy mankind. Not only are these forces unchecked, but their acceleration is still encouraged—even by insurance companies themselves investing the people's money in consequence of this unwholesome crowding.

But in all democratic minds a question now coming uppermost is: what benign power can check such centralization as the city has become—now a destructive fixation?

Well—within the problem itself lies the solution. As always. Centralization itself is the old social principle that made kings an appropriate necessity and is now become the uneconomic force that overbuilt them all, degenerated to a force we call communism. These pseudo-monarchic towns of ours are merely such centralization. Centralization now proves to be something that, used to wind space up tighter and tighter, smaller and higher, is like some centripetal device revolving at increasing speed until—terrible, beyond control—it turns centrifugal, ending all by dispersal or explosion.

Meantime, what possible control?

Government? No—or only to a very limited extent. In democracy, more and more limited to expedients; politics.

The only possible control, then, is profoundly educational. In democracy, is education—when on speaking terms with culture—not the true answer to such exaggerations of artificiality as machine power in production, or as *crowding*? On behalf of humane freedom it is the growth of this human intelligence ultimately applied to the city that must interfere by such pressures as it can exert there where pressure does most good. Salvation from the false economics of centralization lies in wider grasp of the limitations and danger of these powers—machine powers all—multiplied to excess. What hope is there for our future in this machine age, if indeed the machine age is to have any greater future, unless decentralization and appropriate reintegration are soon encouraged—given right-of-way in actual practice?

A Makeshift

Three major artificialities have been drafted and grafted by law upon all modern production; hangovers from petty customs originating in feudal circumstances. Many of these traditions have been blown up into supposed economic patterns: but all forms of rent and all illegitimate. Rent for money; rent for land; really only extrinsic forms of unearned increment; and the third artificiality is traffic in invention. A graft by way of patents is another but less obvious form of "rent."

By mechanical leverage accelerating urban activity, creating pressures never existing before and now never ceasing, these three unnatural economic features are the forces of our present-day city, enormously intensified. Monstrosity has been reached. But the capacity of the human animal for habituation is also enormous—seemingly beyond belief.

32

Rent

The first and most important form of rent contributing to overgrowth of cities, resulting in poverty and unhappiness, is rent for land: land-values created as improvements or by growth, held by some fortuitous fortune's accidental claim to some lucky piece of realty, private but protected by law. Profits from this adventitious form of fortune create a series of white-collarites—satellites of various other unearned increments, like real-estate traffic in more or less lucky land areas. The skyscraper as abused is also an instance of adventitious increment. The city the natural home of this form of "fortune."

The second artificiality: rent for money. By way of the ancient Mosaic invention of "interest," money is now a commodity for sale, so made as to come alive as something in itself—to go on continuously working in order to make all work useless. All profits earned by "big money" are a specious premium placed upon the accretions of labor, creating—in the form of interest—another, a second adventitious form of fortune. More armies of money satellites busily engaged in the sale, distribution, operation and collection of this special form of increment, rent for money, all unearned except as an arbitrary, mysterious premium placed upon money itself "earned," so called by those who made it. A new *speculative commodity* has therefore appeared—money, unnatural as a commodity, now becoming monstrosity. The modern city is its stronghold and chief defender; and insurance is one of its commodities.

The third economic artificiality: unearned increment of the machine itself. The profits of this great, common leverage over labor as now employed by all mankind are thus placed where they seldom, if ever, belong. Here traffic in invention is captained, maintained by a form of capitalism intensified. By the triumph of conscienceless but "rugged individualism" the machine profits of human ingenuity or inspiration in getting the work of the world done are almost all funneled into pockets of fewer and more "rugged" captains-of-industry. Only in a small measure—except by gift or *noblesse oblige* of the captains—are these profits yet (or will they ever be) where they belong; that is to say, with the man whose life is actually modified, given, or sacrificed to this new common agency for doing the work of the world. This agency we call "the machine."

33

So, armies of countless high-powered salesmen—salesmanship the modern art—now come into being in order to unload the senseless overproduction inevitable to this new machine facility, exercised by the hands of insensate "business" greed. The worker is thus dispossessed as owner of the machine: *the man himself,* another dispossession. As subordinate rent-creature, a third form of "fortune" is here. A series of white-collar satellites again rises—selling. This form of propaganda, salesmanship, becomes *the* great modern "art." Politics and journalism (managed publicity) financing, collecting by foreclosure, increasing artificial profits by refinancing, are crafts of repossession. Wholly false fronts are set up as mercantile commonplaces and a wholly false capitalizing of "risk" takes place that now rides high as "insurance." Security not only may be bought but *must* be bought and paid for in almost any case.

Unnatural fixations all—the three economic creatures of rent—all unearned increments. Together with other creatures of false fortune they concentrate money-power in fewer and fewer hands, as insurance. Inevitable centripetal action of capitalistic centralization proceeds by tactfully extended channels of control.

Now, to maintain this mounting external money-power in due force and effect, innumerable legal sanctions must be continuously sought, applied and maintained. Agents of all these artificial factors dovetail together. This is now called the "moral necessity" of "business," until morality is no longer on speaking terms with ethics. What is expedient is too soon legal and enacted by government as moral. What is right (ethical) is entirely another matter, too often beside the mark. Then what is right? What is culture? Where then is this one-time science of human happiness we call "politics"?

Once upon a time the Jeffersonian democratic ideal of these United States was, "that government best government that governs least." But in order to keep the peace and some show of equity between the lower passions so busily begotten in begetting, the complicated forms of super-money-in-crease-money-making and holding are legitimatized by government. Government too, thus becomes monstrosity. Again enormous armies of white-collarites arise. Here comes more bureaucracy: public checking of private money—to add to the public armies of the bureaucrat. All dressed in a little brief authority. As all this comes uppermost major and minor courts are multiplied; petty officials, their complex rulings petrified, become more and more necessary until they, too, are an army keeping tab and collecting "legal" extractions from the citizenry if for no other reason than to maintain such phenomenal bureaucracy. We might now add this form of fortune (the official job) to the other three. But this, too, is only another subordinate creature: government committed to collect rents. Perpetual propaganda becomes a kind of vested interest, itself growing ubiquitous. Again public propaganda perpetrated upon the people for which the people must pay, whether of the minority party or majority party. Always comes the next election and propaganda turned loose.

Multifarious as these laws—enacted by our promise-merchants, the politicians—are, they are only complex expedients to force this swarming clerical breed of bureaucracy to function together. This has bred, finally, still more droves of white-collarites: a new army of lawyers. It becomes impossible to hold, operate, or distribute land, sell or buy money, or manufacture anything, safely, or even marry, make love or die, without the guide and counsel of these specialists in the extraordinary entanglements of rent, of rules, of regulations applied to this or that involute commercial expedient with courts for counters where the attempt to put law above man is made in this complex game we now call our civilization in the prosperity of the machine age. Small wonder, then, that decisions of these specialists in "law and order" so often are themselves in conflict! Lawyers, as satellites of rent, maintain its multiple forms. And so hundreds of thousands of legal experts are the inevitable mentors of whatever mission is now left to the American big city to perform. We must add the lawyer as yet another subordinate form of rent bred by government and thriving upon misfortune or its prevention; but committed, either way, to performance.

These artificialities all depend upon a strong-arm status quo. The Police! Also upon some expedient form of religion wherein men are to be saved (from themselves and each other) and for God by faith in God rather than faith in their own works as men.

All together against quality in these United States, this marching army of quantity is the traditional substitute for organic economic structure of the forms of humane society: art, architecture and religion. Any simple *basis* we might honestly call fundamental to the economy of our democratic republic is not there. This society of ours has overbuilt and now persists in overinhabiting cities—a wholly inorganic basis for survival now shamefully battening upon sources of extrinsic production; senselessly increasing production for the sake of more production! Production is now trying to control consumption—the big horse behind the little cart. This it is that turns the nation into a vast factory, greedy for foreign markets, with the spectre of war as inevitable clearing house.

The old city, already distinctly dated by its own excess, is only further outmoded by every forced increase. Our natural resource now is in new possibilities of access to good uses of good ground: an agronomy intelligently administered.

Our sources of production are intrinsic only with those men who—by skilled or manual toil or concentration of superior ability, by inspiration, upon natural resources or upon actual production whether physical, aesthetic, intellectual, mechanical, or religious—render "value received" to human life. To these hewers of wood and drawers of water and men of the machine, pressing questions of decentralization must be referred. The living, consuming man-unit of our society will ultimately decide this momentous issue. *Consumption must control production.* This matter will only be decided by consumption in proper control of an organic basis for distribution, man to man, nation to nation.

What then of this human subject (or object) the man-unit (he is consumption) upon whom, by his own voluntary subordination, this now vastly complicated uneconomic structure has been erected and cruelly functions, although rudely interrupted by failure about every seven years only to be strong-armed by federal government? Aid. All-pervading, large or small business aid is now quite universally accepted as moral. Even normal?

But what about the man of ideas who labors out of the unknown essential sustenance for all? What about this imaginative individual who gives reality to thought? The planner-designer—he who gets results from materials so far as the life of society is concerned with them? Where in all this is the Artist Agrarian, Artist Mechanic, the inspired Teacher, Inventor, Scientist—

in short, the Artifex? And then what about "hewers of wood, drawers of water, the laborers in the vineyard" and elsewhere?

Well—all are pretty much in the same hard case, or shall we say, caste? No longer masters of fortune. Fear is their daily portion.

Fortunes today engendered (controlled) by schemers; experts in the complex artificialities of this from-the-bottom-to-the-top-down system we are miscalling capitalism. Must this capitalisticism rest upon no broad human basis square with the *nature* of man's rightful relationship to other men or to his own credit here at his own hearth on earth? Facades of false fortune place false premiums upon false traits of his character. Moreover, though the three main systems of false fortune are necessarily maintained by the strong arm of a forced "legitimacy"—that arm, however strong, however reinforced by the police, must periodically tire; come down while confusion and misery of the day of reckoning meantime descend upon all: life itself confused as alarm seeks cover of some kind—somehow—anywhere. We name the chronic recessions thus created (are they a fatal disease?) "depressions." Or, if it is a managed convulsion by high-powered finance, we have war: war the inevitable clearing house of finance-a-la-mode: always war! Nothing else can save any system from destruction where production controls consumption except it be by this ages-old destroyer. War.

Where, then, in this destructive ambush of strong-arm-artificiality superimposed on artificiality, is integrity of the genuine artifex to be found? Where is the original source—basic master of ideas—inspiring the artifex? What place has he in this economic Tower of Babel with its apex in false fortune; accelerating manufacture for exaggerated profits? All profiteering— a deflation of manhood to inflate and exploit mankind. Inflation is bound to be characteristic of any such haphazard system strong-armed by law. Why miscall this system Capitalism when its base is up in air and apex down on the ground?

The Artifex

We admit that such haphazard centralization as we have attempted in utter materialism confers certain human benefits upon the artifex, stimulating by financial reward his ingenuity in machine development and all its uses. But far more extensive uses of our vast machine resources now do lie ready to make life more available to the citizen. Meantime, essential right-mindedness and decency of the artifex have moved him to go on working in this confusion of our machine age; trying to cultivate justice, generosity, and pity; best of all, the beauty of individual responsibility—in the midst of chaos. Upstream almost all the way without very well knowing why or how, worshipping not a golden god hidden in a cave but a great spirit ruling all by Principle. Modern man has been doing so without quite knowing how to apply that inner principle; hardly knowing even in just what the principle really consists.

Nevertheless, he knows that god of the free artifex is a great free Spirit allowing man to choose between what is good *for* him and good *in* him as against what is bad *in* him and bad *for* him, so that by free exercise of his conscience he may himself grow god-like. The road to a good life is still open to the artifex. But today his road must lead on through persistent public obstruction, most of all the drift toward conformity—the subtle envious propaganda against superiority—hindrances legally erected, legalities exploiting his good faith—a general depravity in a drift toward quantity at expense to quality, until we find all heading in toward war or revolution: this time the revolution industrial—yes. Agrarian, no. About time now our agronomy asserted itself in his behalf. You've left a glimmer still to cheer the man—the artifex—and by that light now mark my words we'll build the perfect ship.—(Kipling's McAndrew's Hymn.)

An Experiment

In spite of all perversity—of the cash-and-carry mentality, the servile system it would maintain (if it could) grafted upon the new world of organic character—appears this modern organic concept of man and his God as organic growth: therefore a deeper sense of human integrity which we might properly call organic Democracy. Out of this philosophic romance, the life of man began with this new nation of ours as a foundling conceived in liberty to pursue the growth we call happiness. All men to have equal opportunity before the law; thus to develop manhood. Our vast territory, riches untouched, was inherited by all breeds of the earth who were courageous enough to come and take domain on the hard terms of "pioneer." A new frontier we erected then. Not the frontier we are facing now.

Our new nation, called a republic, was an experiment in freedom, eagerly manned by refugees from the despotism and monarchy of all nations. Soon we became a great federation of states, the greatest known—these United States of America. United, the states became a nation—call it Usonia— harboring within its borders the murderer, the adventurer, the outcast, the cheated, the thwarted and the superior: the predatory worst but also the courageous best of human kind deserting previous nationality to make a new nation—a life there to be in the image of a great ideal of freedom—at home on vast incomparable ground. Or so its leaders planned, hoped and pleaded. A new nation founded upon the best and the worst wherein rule by the bravest and the best would be *natural*.

Though with no corresponding revisions of traditional, Romish, or feudal, property-rights; and not much, if any, consideration given to appropriate new economy, our new country *was* founded upon a more just freedom for the individual than any before known: "that government best government which governs least" said a Thomas Jefferson crossing an Alexander Hamilton. George Washington, Thomas Paine, Abraham Lincoln, William Lloyd Garrison, John Brown, Emerson, Whitman, Thoreau, Henry George, Louis Sullivan—such as these and their kind were her sons. In them the original ideal was held clear. Then arose indiscriminate private wealth by way of fortuitous survivals of despotisms: feudal money-getting and property-holding. The new nation carelessly adopted them. An economic order more suited to monarchy and despotism than freedom was let loose with fresh ascendancy. Now see a new free-for-all race for power of riches, riches of power. It soon outran such culture as appeared, or bought it ready-made. Unnatural reservoirs of capital as predatory accumulation made away with

39

what little cultural understanding the new country had originally borrowed —a culture of no indigenous integrity. It was easy to discover, gather and exploit the fresh spoils of our vast new territory that huge fortunes piled up, almost overnight, in hands least fitted to administer the powers of wealth. The fortunate, lucky, were only too willing to buy ready-made whatever they might like—buy what they did not know they could only have truly if *grown*. Suddenly rich, not content within the culture they had with them (or on them) when they came here, they were quite satisfied with importation they could buy. As a matter of course the original idea of Freedom grew thin so far as culture went, and grew dim or died. Such arts as had come to our new states with the frugal decency of the early colonials survived but a short time, but there was no principle originally involved, or living, in the Colonial arts that came over to grow new culture upon. Originally modified French elegance or borrowed Italian Renaissance, they were already degenerate when they reached new land. Soon with the advent of so many foreign nationalities came licentious eclecticisms in all art. By way of peripatetic taste we were especially devastated in architecture. A ready-made art, antique or pseudo-classic (the same thing), satisfied the pressing social demand and even became the pressing need of Society in the new nation. Riches in general so rapidly overwhelmed any indigenous culture that so-called "American architecture" fell to the great low in eclecticism of all time. "Culture" attempted thus ready-made became a mere commodity. So its merchant became "moral." The merchant became desirable, even a social-aesthete! To refer to Principle was not yet offensive to science, but it was peculiarly offensive to the merchant in the education of the arts. To refer whatever culture we had to Principle was then beside the mark. The "radical" became an offense: dangerous! Where there were no roots, why look for them as he would? The radical became a menace, considered—even as now—unconstitutional.

Here (is it for the first time in history?) a self-determining polyglot people on incomparable ground, subscribing to the highest ideal of human freedom yet known, sprang into being as a nation with a curious bastardized culture; its culture a quarreling collection of many ready-made cultures of the world, borrowed, pieced together by uncultivated "taste." Such as it was, here was a makeshift garment worn outside in—even upside down— not cast away as we now see it should have been. So we got the wasteful makeshift our eclecticisms became and that we now regard in this ugly discord all around us. Incongruity was begot by riches. Great abortion. But abortion was merchantable, therefore "moral," no more than a makeshift; a purchase consisting at best in some copy of the great rebirth called "the Renaissance" so that nothing indigenous in art could be born to us. Thus quondam bastardization of the new nation's character was artificially elected and applied; an artificiality soon to be confirmed by "higher" education! Education in America became a collection of imported academic devices arbitrarily applied to the surface of life. And, too soon, the authority of this pseudo-culture was battening upon developments of our material resources, characterizing our wealth. Externally applied substitutes such as these inevitably failed to inspire an appropriate (Usonian) way of life of our own —or of our era—or to encourage integrity in interpretation of our new ideal of freedom; the ideal upon which the life of our new country was so eagerly founded: the Sovereignty of the Individual!

So this new nation arose, grew in might as it grew in riches but, so far as culture went, shamefully wasting, upon the imported substitute, its every natural characteristic and resource. Strange perversions or absurd pretenses were presented as worthy.

But the nation quickly outgrew the narrow bounds of the weak borrowed forms, even while academic education still continued to condition the people by planting and nursing the Substitute. See the buildings they built for the purpose. No constructive lessons could be learned from such servile eclecticism as became nationally characteristic. All our great nation had upon which to found and grow indigenous culture was sacrificed to this reflection of the "setting sun all Europe had mistaken for dawn." Academic abnegation amounted to obsession; and, by the personal likes or dislikes of the wives of our rugged culture-puzzled individualists who themselves really cared nothing at all about the matter, art became a mere academic pretense or a fashion; American culture a form of license putting on provincial airs and fancified attire.

This pseudo-culture became the more deplorable as our money-power grew more enormous. The better citizenry—north, south, east, west—took refuge in the authentic antique, and committed aesthetic suicide by acquiring monstrosities openly in the name of the "classic." Conformity. Mere names and "the styles" thus gained prestige and, soon, authority. Periodic fashion could, and did, rule supreme. Downright imitation in all arts that should have been creative became at least honorable though impotent. This very impotence was called "conservative!" Meantime the more fancified citizenry also committed promiscuous adultery by the purchase of atrocities in the name of the Louis' and their mistresses. Paris was capital not only of the pseudo-English Colonial venture in culture; it now became the capital of our own pseudo-aesthetic interests.

This prostitute pictorial performance was, in our national life, raised to authorized academic pattern, eagerly grasped and sanctioned by the Mrs. Gablemores and Madame Plasterbilts of American "good society." Evil consequences of this confusion or degradation of choice by what the selective "taste" of the period could buy abroad—or import—were fashionable.

The god of Principle to guide the rulers of the country new-founded upon a more just expression of human liberty than men had known before did not seem to inspire appropriate (or even sensible) interpretations for the ways and means of the free and democratic life that had been made possible. Nor did the wealthy or the supremely successful seem to understand not only what life under their great democratic ideal meant in terms of economics, but not at all what arts or crafts would be natural to such a life as ours. Unsuitable fruits of the old monarchic-authoritarian system prevailed, demoralizing any vital functioning of art. So also demoralized whatever else went with it? Ancient "traditions" now entered the heart of the nation. Not in spirit? No. As culture, a mere eclecticism damnable by taste. In place of culture of our own came servile abnegation to the past. We were conservative?

Architecture, parasitism for five centuries, sank to incontinent imitation by our ever freshly confirmed eclectic fashionables. Religion itself (quite naturally) sank beneath the level of duly accredited servility. The need to maintain this abnegation or sterilization was inevitable. In all valid interests of our new life, exploitation of the cliché (the "formula") in religion as well as aesthetics had right of way because get-rich-quick patrons found it as expedient to get-culture-quick. Yes . . . ignorant provincial social ambitions

42

had found this cheap shortcut to culture. The healthy spiritual significance of our own new ideal of freedom—Democracy—was, and so easily, betrayed by the powers of financial success.

Provincial people thus superficially and suddenly eclectified could, perhaps, breed "tastes" that could only turn back to taste—instead of growing new life of the spirit or new ground in a new era. The culture we as a people needed was a culture the European world itself needed in somewhat different terms.

So, once again, this time in the latter days of the nineteenth century and early in the twentieth, our American academic world mistook the setting sun for dawn. "*Pseudo*" by official order was duly confirmed as Precedent and ruled over popular education. "American" in culture became the highly respectable following-after into general outer darkness which we now see in perspective as the present "International" cliché.

The Culture Lag

What could such superartificiality do but stumble and fall wherever or whenever Life insisted upon itself as beautiful?

The cultural lag? The lag was to be proudly worn as a tag of respectability for another half-century before it became a rag.

Still with us now, to stay perhaps for some years more? Still with us though modified—at least by mouth.

There could be nothing of course in such bottoms-up provincial servility as ours that could grow anything at all worthy of the spirit of our great adventure? Wealth, indiscriminate, and growing abuse of vicarious power, increased the numbers of those unqualified for success; and the new country could only outgrow old medieval cities—centralization patterned after the ancient feudal town outmoded. That appropriate beautiful town now became static. The great ideal of Freedom had declined, by the refusal of "authority" to let it be truly free. Money-power could not be substituted for ideas, could do no more than make more money with money or go to war. Go to war it went.

The Jeffersonian democratic ideal, so inspiring in the beginning, is really the highest form of aristocracy this world has ever seen: aristocracy genuinely a quality of the man himself—not merely bestowed upon him by heredity or privilege: now a matter of *character*.

But aristocracy lacked spiritual nourishment and man had grown sterile. He had little left that could encourage and give prestige to the new idea of democracy. And so old intellectual equipment met new paraphernalia head on. Indigenous culture was—to this day—left to languish. Except as the cultural mask might be imposed by architects—themselves no more than drapers and haberdashers of the arts—shallow *couturiers* who functioned as "artists." High-powered salesmanship by professionally managed publicity was able to sell their feeble or profane derivations of old culture to new "success"—if not shameful ugliness, sheer stupidity—and any upsurge of vitality in the arts of the new republic was left to lie before us. Reproach growing to this day! Naked necessity would have been far better.

This cultural mask has thus covered and concealed our true nature. In the name of some bad forms of surface-decoration, or the cliché internationale, our country was and still is being taught to call it Architecture. All but one of our universities have conditioned the novitiate to regard this bastardization of motive as the essence of art and architecture.

So the teenager—American youth—goes to the stocks to be conditioned by false qualifiers in the greatest eclecticisms of all time—our big colleges. There hopelessly confirmed parasites of the American spirit teach our youth. They are crammed with imported formulas for all this idiosyncrasy of "good taste." But taste can never be more than a matter of ignorance now, because the way to knowledge is truly open to the teenager.

Such substitute for culture—suitably urban—as we have set up in the big cities of these United States, thus betrays the country. It functions as something imposed upon American life because we—the people—could not or would not learn the value of culture really grown out of the daily circumstances of our life. Organic. Unable to live our own lives where the fruits of a new civilization might be our concern we have found it so much easier —cheaper too—to fake our culture, or buy it ready-made. Uncertain pro-

44

vincials, still awkward, we have been afraid of being laughed at if our "choice" (taste) should happen not to be properly certified by duly managed prestige. In our ignorance, such *authority* was once upon a time all we had to *steer* by.

For the Individual

Buddha believed in nonvicarious effort—the spirit—only; that is to say, only in effort disciplined from within. The individual himself might never reach the ultimate for man on earth but what matter?

And Jesus taught the dignity and worth of the individual as developed from within. *"The Kingdom of God is within you"*: the potential of individuality. Christianity in his name diverted this teaching, professionalized and confused it in creeds and churches. Even by the Gothic cathedrals.

The Church, with its creeds that Jesus did not want, discounted his Idea, seeing in it only "every man for himself and the devil for the hindmost." So "religion" has too often emphasized the desirability of the disappearance of individuality: this, more or less, is also the politics of fascism or of communism; similar to the practice of monarchic, socialistic or communistic peoples. Meantime the protestant succeeded in bringing individuality back, but only partially; as a compromised Ideal.

Some five hundred years before the life of Jesus, the Chinese philosopher Laotze preached the sense of Individuality as a reflex of the organic unity of the Cosmos: the true source of human power, the all pervasive "state-of-becoming!" Our own democratic ideal of the social state seems originally conceived as some such unity. That is to say, Democracy was conceived as the free growth of humane individuality, mankind free to function together in unity of spirit (their own skill in the making); by nature thus averse to formalism and so to institutionalizing. Institution seemed a form of death. This ideal of Nature lies at the core of organic democracy, and architecture organic. We should emphasize this in order to regain ground lost to the industrial revolution and consequent wars. But now come haphazard big builders of these haphazard cities being badly overbuilt. By way of the industrial revolution this great iron horse (the Machine), upon which the

West rode to power, is now rampant in the Middle East and the East. The yellow man, ubiquitous, is learning to ride. Well, why are we afraid of him? Is it our conscience? Or the lack of it?

Out of American "rugged individualism" captained by rugged captains of our rugged industrial enterprises we have gradually evolved a crude, vain power: plutocratic "Capitalism." Not true capitalism. I believe this is entirely foreign to our own original idea of Democracy. The actual difference between such "individualism" and individuality of true democracy lies in the difference between cowardly selfishness and noble selfhood! Like the difference between sentiment and sentimentality or the difference between liberty and license.

"Isms" only aggravate misuse of vicarious powers by our expedient masters of the expedient, using the three great increments—rent for land, rent for money, and rent for manhood—to put native individuality into bad repute, or into its grave. Like the abuse of any good thing abuses of individuality will bring reactionary consequences. Proof of such reaction is with us today. Fearful, our ultra-conservative rich men are proof enough. But our art, degraded to the level of the makeshift, and our tottering religion, are stronger proof. These personal idiot-syncrasies of "the man of taste" by which we are persistently misled in the name of individuality are still more evidence. If creative ability is our concern, we may be seen to have failed, because sterility has been the natural consequence of vicarious exercise of our enormous mechanical powers. Abuses of power are characteristics of ultimate defeat. Not success. Quantity uprises at expense to quality. This is surely the antithesis of Democracy.

But true creative ability as always will be the first concern of democratic individuality. And, conversely, Individuality must ever be the concern and success of creative ability. Until Usonia recognizes individuality not as personality merely but as the natural blossom and fruit of organic character; seldom if ever common; always radical—therefore, however difficult, is conservative of Life itself (being *of* the Soul)—we will have no adequate share in Democracy nor any in its defense, because we will not have grasped what Democracy really means! Then how can we learn to develop and protect it if we do not learn to know what it does really mean?

46

Democracy cannot afford mere personality to be mistaken for true human individuality. Nor can the human will and mere intellect ever produce true individuality. Any such attempt could make only a mimic, or a monster; perhaps at best a scientist. Should our own great or near-great ever become able to draw the line between the Curious and the Beautiful, this difference between personality and individuality will come clear. Salvation of our culture therefore lies in practices which would be evident enough if we would evolve true definitions of the character of our purpose and the nature of our circumstances.

We "the Free" should recognize individuality as organic entity of the man: essence of the soul of true manhood. Democracy is of the soul, not an expedient. Our policy would then always be a determination to struggle against any form of fixation or conformity. Militocracy or any cliché outside that of the machine itself would be murder of opportunity.

If the significance (*spirit*) of form is lacking, creative art can be nothing of or for the soul. Only where this significance is the aura of form does the spirit enter into man-made things. Art. To be insignificant our nation needs only to be without this radiant aura of indigenous spirit. To be a people without this supreme poetic expression of principle—Art and Architecture— is to be untrue to our ideology, untrue to ourselves. To have no true philosophy as sanctuary for the spirit of Freedom is to have no haven for genius, national or personal.

Democratic individuality therefore may be said to be organic; of the character of the "person" or of "things." An inner *quality*. So we may properly call that *quality* as of the Soul. Creative manhood, first to last, is concerned with soul as the deeper significance. Education should consist in learning to recognize its integrity and this indigenous character wherever found in people or things. When we speak of character we often really refer to individuality. Democracy is the very gospel of Individuality.

Without such elemental human integrity, there can be only the use and abuse of materialism not much above the belt, and vicarious. That is to say not above artificiality. No great art or architecture, as poetry; no religion; no integrity even of conduct.

If we deeply enough desire democracy, we will be much more careful of how we turn upon our basic ego—selfhood—just because we have failed to distinguish it from mere egotism. We have misnamed so many flagrant abuses by egotism in the name of individuality. For instance the rugged "individualism" of capitalism. "Capitalistic" may mean merely individual-*ism,* or a run-in with riot. Such ism may be (usually is) completely something else—something for which true individuality has but scorn. And true individuality has no more to do with the crass methods of mercantile egotism such as ours than with communism or socialism at its other extreme. Democratic individuality, a salient essence of all human life, is the fundamental core of Art and Artist—creative.

No isms can express true individuality. Any man with a formula instead of a spirit has already taken his place as an affront to nature: a mere *substitute* no matter what ist, ism, or ite he may be.

> "Man, proud man,
> Drest in a little brief authority,
> Most ignorant of what he's most assured,
> His glassy essence, like an angry ape,
> Plays such fantastic tricks before high heaven,
> As make the angels weep."

Great religious leaders—Buddha, Jesus, Abdul Bahai, Mohammed, Laotze especially—wanted no formalism by institutionalizing religion: tolerated no bureaucracy or officialism in the realm of the Spirit. Such integrity of soul wanted not even disciples!

So human nature, far "out of drawing" in this day of our own time, is bound to miseducate because miseducated. The education that would be essential to the freedom of human nature is either on crutches now or pitifully weak; pseudo-functioning only on pseudo lines; staying on the boulevard; thinking by the groove; moving by interior wheels or on rails. City pavements? The sidewalk-happy probably function best when off hard pavements and in the rut. And, since we all go now on wheels on rail or pavement, or "fly," life tends to become a rut. So rut-government seems inevitable at the moment and the rut the "way of all flesh."

48

How then does the rut become disreputable? Surely expedient, considered moral, therefore it is said to be safe—"conservative." Often it is only the rut that we call Law and Order. May it be what we are now inclined to call civilization?

So Individuality *is* a menace to all forms of rut-life. Rut-life turns with ratlike perspicacity against all individuality; with hatreds born of Fear. The so-called Conservative has always hated the Radical: hates him with good reason because the "conservative" is afraid of going to the roots of anything at all—just because he knows instinctively he has no roots! And there can be none wherever he is on the ground.

Now, we are here reading an actual consideration of the nature of the future city of democracy: a city with greater future for human individuality: a life in deeper organic sense, true to man's own Spirit—individuality being *fundamental integrity of the soul of man* in his own time and place—and so most valuable asset of the human race. Without this city of its own America will never have known a culture of its own. No great architecture can arise *from* us or *for* us based upon the expedient use of the ancient city. Wherever there will be the democratic city, individuality of conscience and the conscience of individuality will be inviolate.

The Inexorable Law of Change

We must admit that before the advent of any wholesale standardized mechanization of a new city the American way of life in the old city was, in its effects and proportions, no longer humane because its basic plan was so completely medieval. The Middle Ages.

In no planning which the old city has received has modern spacing been based fairly enough upon the new time scale of modern mobilization—the human being no longer on his feet or seated in a trap behind a horse or two, but in his motor car, or going in his plane. Listening to commentators on the subject, we find that machinery has brought to us no alternative plan. Urban life, originally, was a festival of wit, a show of pomp and a revel of occasion while all was still in *human scale*. True urbanization rewarded life back there in feudal circumstances, a life for which our cities of today were originally planned and built, formed by and for a group-life of powerful individualities, themselves in scale true to human life in medieval times. Then conveniently enough spaced. But now under modern machine age pressures, the better life is being driven, or wills itself, away. Either gone or going now, it travels to and fro: perhaps lives in penthouses in the city or far beyond in country estates. More time wasted in the to and fro than is spent in desirable activity. Such genius as the big city now knows is recruited from farms and villages of the American countryside. No city with over 100,000 population can live by its own birthrate. The recruits, celebrants of the hard pavement (such as they are), sidewalk-happy, all now seek the city to find it to be a market only: insatiable. A great maw demanding and devouring *quantity* instead of encouraging and protecting *quality*. As it devours man, so now it must devour itself. Fish are for sale in this marketplace but there are none in its streams. The foolish celebrant, crowding in on crowds of hypnotized seekers no less confused, frequently escapes to the countryside; escape essential because the overgrown city now offers him nothing he cannot better find on terms of comparative health and freedom in the beauty of the countryside. Already the age of the machine has laid that open to "his majesty the American citizen." While he slept it came upon him . . . the American architect notwithstanding—impotent.

Again, reflect upon these facts: first the fundamental unit of space-measurement in modern life has, for every man, so radically changed that he now bulks twenty to one—even a hundred to one—when he gets around about seated in his favorite motor car. Then reflect that mobilization has only just begun! This circumstance of the car alone is rendering the old big city obsolete? Like some hopelessly inadequate old boat or building, the city itself is still in use, inhabited because we feel we cannot afford to throw it away and allow the spirit of Time, Place, and Man to build the new ones we now so much need. Soon we will be willing to give all we have to get on with the well-planned city of our own freedom. Inevitably this new city is underway for our posterity if not for ourselves. Posterity must have it.

But reading history we learn that the devouring of human individuality has ended invariably in eventual desolation together of the devourer and

50

the devoured. Once render conscience "suspect" or deny conscience as sacred to freedom itself and you have only downfall ahead: of man or his works.

Then why and for what are these overgrown American cities so desperately maintained? Exaggerated as they now are, and held against the normal tide of change? Held for militocracy, prostitution, banking and war? At what price?

Illusion

And yet, coming to the greatest of them, New York, for the first time, one has the illusion that we must be a great people to have raised this heavy barrage of relentless commercial mantraps so high; to have grandly hung so much book-architecture upon cumbrous old-fashioned steel framing, so regardless. Inhabited at such enormous cost not alone in money but in all human values as well.

Such frantic energy pours through this haphazard money-mountain made by the mile to pile up and confuse men and materials, haphazard; here and there ruthless; drenched by what relentless ambition has wrung from our abounding national resources. Well, what of it—if everywhere these resources are wasted by foolish attempts at establishment by the nation and we end in some form of bad surface-decoration? What if one arrogant skyscraper does outrun or ram another, and crams the horizon with harsh haphazard masses—upended, crowding on the bewildered wistful eye, peering up from black shadows cast upon the man down there below on hard pavement? What, if so? We have seen crowding, greater if similar, as destructive drama wherever irresistible physical force has violated mankind or tilted up and broken through earth's crust. So—see in this volcanic crater of confused energy bred by money-power, no wise control of enormous mechanical forces, pushing up to crowd and be crowded, to grind against each other with a blind force moved by common greed. Crowded exploitation, as only the Machine can crowd and exploit, forcing *anxiety* upon all modern life. Is astonishment at all this akin to admiration? But consider— this is never a *noble* expression of life; it is again and again only the apotheosis by the gregarious expedient of overmastering Rent.

THE OLD CITY

The shadows of these haphazard skyscrapers cast down below are significant. Their shadows are the surviving shadow-of-the-ancient-wall of the cave-dweller.

The skyscraper if considered as independent achievement in itself may be justifiable: a prideful thing! A tall building may be very beautiful, economical and desirable in itself—provided always that it is in no way interference with what lives below, but looking further ahead than the end of the landlord's ruse—by inhabiting a small green park. That park is humane now. The skyscraper is no longer sane unless in free green space. In the country it may stand beautiful for its own sake.

52

Exaggerated perpendicularity has no such bill-of-health. It is now the the terrible stricture of our big city. Whatever is perpendicular casts a shadow: shadows of the skyscraper fall aground and where crowded are an utterly selfish exploitation. Because, if the civic rights of the neighbor down there below, in the shadows, were to be exercised, there would be no "skyscraping" at all. There would be only a general rise in urban floor-level. Without much sense and with no distinction, cramping and swamping all tenantry in artificial light and forced ventilation, all would congest and be congestion unbearable even to the herd-struck morons our present sky-scraperism has cultivated.

The Light of Day

So to the urban skyscraper-builder in overcrowded cities the very inso-lence of the urban skyscraper-feat is no small measure of its attraction? Although skyscraperism fits so well into the primitive psychology of the "rugged individualist" of the industrial revolution—he who from an office fifty stories above the man in the street casts his ominous shadow below upon the man he directs in some great money-making enterprise—he *is* "success?" He is at last picturesque in the way he likes to be. The tall silk hat and gold-tipped stick of the past had only a little something to gratify his old-fashioned equivalent—but now? What a hallmark, the very tallest building in the big city outcrowding the already overcrowded, based upon commercial success! Ancient titles? Mere nicknames! Here he is—the tangi-ble proof of the "greatness" of modern business. In the city, is this sky-scraper shadow his own shadow? But what does that matter or mean to his place in Time? He will never know.

Now move him and his shadow into the open spaces and he becomes truly splendid: a contribution to the glory and dignity of our era. The difference?

Simple. As material things stand with us today the skyscraper might be ultimate expression of the individuality fairly expected from the freedom of democracy to signify what we have so painstakingly prophesied and now discourage. But in the overcrowded big city it is no exalted order of merit.

54

See it there as conspicuous proof of the cultural lag and a fine example of our conspicuous waste.

In the present era's future (if it has one) the skyscraper will be considered *"ne plus ultra* of the *e pluribus unum"* capitalistic centralization. The New York skyscraper will be seen as the prancing of this great iron horse—the industrial revolution. The iron horse rearing high hoofs in air for the plunge before the runaway—the runaway to oblivion by way of the atom bomb—or we go to the country!

Thus enforced upon our understanding by the non-understanding in overgrown urban life, skyscraping is not merely a falsity but a moral, economic, aesthetic, ethical monstrosity!

This exaggeration of privilege among us is already far out of democratic scale. Owing to social, collegiate, and commercial pride of exploitation going hand in hand with miseducation—if properly citified, "well mechanized," that is to say standardized by commerce, the citizen is now so far gone that he easily mistakes the pig-piling and crowding of big business for eminence of excellence: mistakes the pushbutton powers of the machine age for his own powers and finds hectic excitement in urban uproar and the vertigo of verticality. The more citified he becomes the less civilized he is; the more this racing of the iron-horse into the inferiority of conformity grows characteristic of his weakness. Roaring tumults of congestion emphasize terrific collisions of power; explosions of grinding mechanical forces in this whirling vortex, urban exaggeration; in these the rich whirling-dervish thinks he sees *his own* greatness. In the whirl the citizen is satiated—his "greatness" something wholly vicarious. But his shadow too is the shadow cast by the sun.

And yet—seen at night, heedless of stampede, the haphazard monster has myriad beauties of silhouette; light streaming—the light punctuated by reflected or refracted lights. In human terms yet undefined, the nocturnal monster yields rhythmical perspectives, glowing spotted walls of light, dotted lines, a world of fascinating reflections hung upon other reflections ranging along vistas of the street or pendent as the wisteria hangs its violet racemes on a trellis or the trees. Then the skyscraper is, in the dusk, a shimmering, prismatic verticality; gossamer veil of a festive scene, hanging there against the backdrop of a black night sky to dazzle, entertain, and amaze, in great masses. Lighted interiors come through the veil with a sense of life and well-being. The City then seems alive. It does live as illusion lives.

The light of day? Streams of more and more insignificant facades and dead walls rise and pour out of hard faced masses behind and above human beings all crawling on hard pavements like ants to "hole in" somewhere or find their way to this or that cubicle. Beings packed into the roar, rush and danger of a new kind of the old voracity—speed. And out of other holes everywhere elsewhere pour these sordid reiterations, rent, rented, or in pursuit of rent! Overpowering emphasis everywhere of the cell in upended stricture; continual slicing, edging, inching in all the crowding. Tier above tier rises the soulless habitation of the shelf. Interminable empty crevices run up and down the winding ways of windy unhealthy canyons. Heartless, this now universal grip of grasping, unending stricture. Box to box on box boxing, glassed in boxing looking into other glass-boxing. Black shadows falling on glass fronts with artificial lights burning behind them day long. Millions upon millions of little cavities, cells squared by the acre, acreage spread by the mile. This a vast prison with glass fronts.

Above this avaricious aggregation which cruel ambition has built and now patronizes are haphazard odd insignificant skylines: like the false ambitions below making it all more human by lying about it. Elaborate ornamentation is all spasmodic. Here goes and comes to go again the to-and-fro, anxiety, satiety of life in the machine age. Incessant the wear of the cities, always to stop-and-go, go-and-stop only to crisscross again. Every human movement made is made to be broken! Every human being's interest, private interest, is entangled and in danger everywhere. Every heart that beats—beaten soon or late.

Streets? All too narrow channels jammed and jamming traffic. When available they are all, at best, only half effective owing to the ubiquitous crisscross of the gridiron. Always the gridiron! Forever a bedlam of harsh, torturing shrieks and roars. This wasteful spasm of racing movement to and fro in the crisscross. Down erstwhile narrow old village lanes one is deep in dark shadows cast by distorted forces. Therein lurk the ambitions and frustrations of the human being urbanized out of scale with its own body. Here see defeat of all aspirations of the human heart. The sense of humane proportion lost.

Incongruous mantrap of monstrous dimensions! Enormity devouring manhood, confusing personality by frustration of individuality? Is this not Anti-Christ? The Moloch that knows no God but *more?*

The agonizing traffic problem is here seen forced upon the city originally made and now aggravated by the persistent landlord with his skyscraper. The present city is yet only about one-tenth the motor car city it must become within the next fifteen years unless the citizen abandons his car. But dutiful devotion to advantages of our machine age now means to every citizen either a motor car—or two or three—(comparative flight) a helicopter; or else a frustrated moron for a citizen. Or a maniac? Every citizen will have a car or two or already dreams of having more, meantime envying the neighbor his four. Three, two or one—observe if the new free-way or the gridiron congestion is not already crucifixion. Then what comes, as average success multiplies and relentlessly multiplies the excess of our already excessive mechanical leverage?

Roughly calculate the mass of public conveyances, taxicabs, buses, private cars and trucks that success will bring to any overgrown village consisting of one hundred thousand to several million people: add half that number of private cars and add, perhaps one twenty-fifth as many delivery machines; add one fiftieth as many buses to displace streetcar tracks and carry children to school; and add unwholesome subways. You will find that—with room enough for each incidental transient coming into town from the suburbs (or going out), in order to function at all lengthwise, to say nothing of around about or crosswise—the surging maniacal mass inextricable would pig-pile in the narrow channels of the city well above the seventh story!

Allowing now for the established urban crisscross (the gridiron making every city street only half-time efficient) the struggling mass would again double; pile up and submerge even the ten-story buildings? Call this exaggeration: cut it in two. Then, if you like, cut it in two again. There will still be enough cars pounding along the streets and pouring carbon monoxide into them to put Manhattan and all its kind completely out of commission, starved for oxygen.

Now consider the fact that motorcar traffic has just begun within this resurrection of ancient Bedlam. Then why deck, double-deck, or triple-deck city streets or burrow in holes below them at a cost of billions only to invite further increase and eventually inevitable defeat? Now see these new imitations of old feudal cities as total loss to modern times.

Why not then allow the citizenry to keep the billions they would have to pay for decking and burrowing? They could buy more and better cars and perhaps soon safe flying machines, eventually bailing out of the urban mantrap into the more natural life of the small town fruitfully expanded in the country. As the freedom of our democracy dawns genuine in the citizen's heart, the present prison-city vanishes by way of its own senseless excess. Hazardous machine power built the excess and, if left haphazard, will ruin it. A City should now be the planned consequence of better understanding of what the nature of the machine may mean to the man with a conscience; and this must now be made constructive. Without this integrity on our part our boasted democratic freedom is going—going—something soon doomed entirely by its own foolish extravagant ignorance—and gone.

So no longer manifest is any clear thought or sane feeling for humane good in urban exaggeration. Humane elements are sterilized by it or demoralized. Lurking in sinister urban shadows cast by these prideful urban strictures, lie the legalised impositions of today; and no less in our libraries, museums, colleges and in institutions of learning and especially of authority —a terrifying make-believe. The abortion we see in street facades has become a general frown. This surviving shadow of the ancient wall itself sinister. Savage or unsane as the convulsions caused by the overgrown city are—we see in them as valid an example of deterioration by "advantages" as has existed in all time.

Just because we have some little thriving village of yesterday (port perhaps) driven thus mad by excess—why is it so conveniently mistaken for principles? Success creative would seldom if ever know! The abnormality the city breeds is nothing more than much more of the already much-too-much in all the hell there is right now!

THE FIREPROOF UNIFIED FARM BUILDING FOR SMALL ACREAGE FARMS

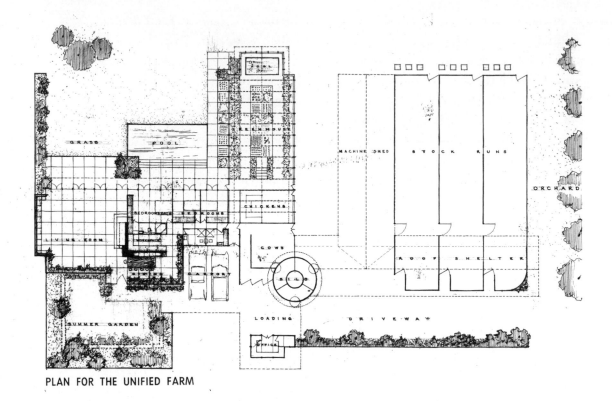

PLAN FOR THE UNIFIED FARM

Forces Tearing the Vortex Down

Human sensibilities, above the belt, are growing tired or numb. But good hope lies in this fact: this whole swollen commercial enterprise we call the City proceeds to stall its own engine by its owners' own excess. The day of reckoning is not so far away.

Mercantile interests have overbuilt the city, own it, and are now spending billions to keep it in place and going, using such man-prowess as we have to make ground-rent, floor-rent, man-rent and money-rent acceptable to urban millions; all, including themselves now, in immediate danger of running each other down in a race for bigger and better bait for no less acquisitive but even more bewildered tenants.

60

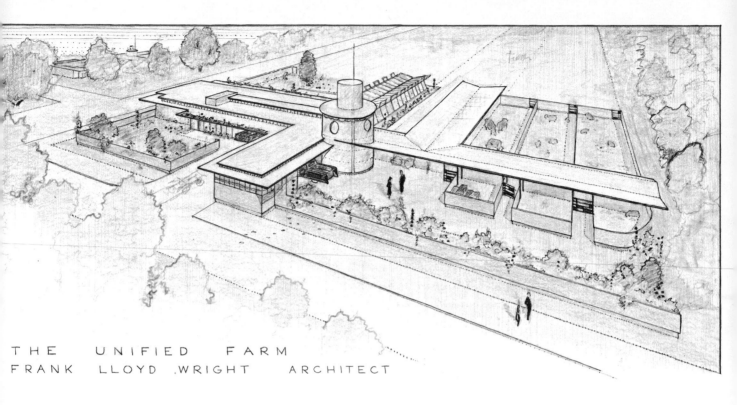

THE   UNIFIED   FARM
FRANK   LLOYD   WRIGHT   ARCHITECT

So inexorable forces that have overbuilt the city for swarming tenantry in so many different forms, yet all the same, build and build only to see urban monstrosity tear itself down or wear itself out by its own overweight: obesity is not yet a virtue.

For a page or two now let us examine these inimical mechanical forces, thrusting against human life by all this vain exaggeration and try to see just how natural forces may return all festering excess to the soil. If humanity were only there on its own inheritance—this good ground—cancerous overgrowth, wrought upon the life of these United States, might be gradually healed. The small home-farm-building to take the place of promiscuous farm buildings and the tenement is one item in sight shown in detail by the drawings of Broadacres: free city.

61

Of all the underlying forces working toward emancipation of the city dweller, most important is the gradual reawakening of the primitive instincts of the agrarian. Agronomy, source of the ancient wandering tribe. The adventurer down the ages reappears, his instinct still intermingling with the static of the cave-dweller. Call the survival of the ancient feudal city due to survival of the ancient cave-dweller instinct. The adventurer protests and denies this surviving shadow-of-the-wall—this old new city.

Physical forces of the machine itself, electrical, mechanical, and chemical invention, are meantime volatilizing human movement, voice and vision.

62

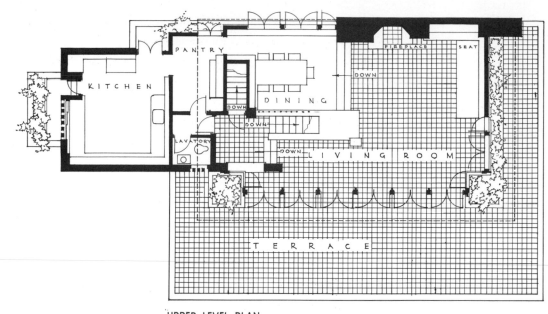

KITCHEN

PANTRY

DINING

DOWN

FIREPLACE   SEAT

DOWN

DOWN

LAVATORY

DOWN   LIVING   ROOM

TERRACE

UPPER LEVEL PLAN

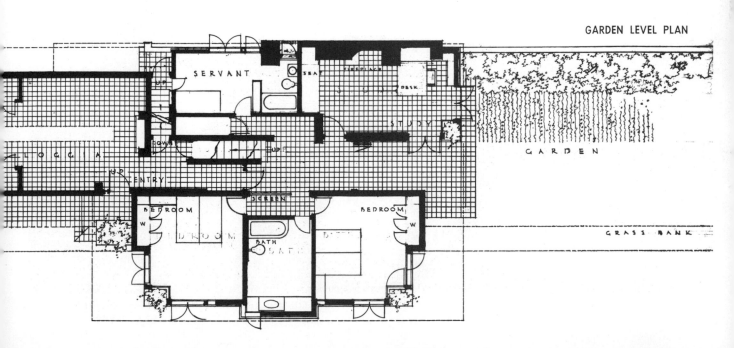

GARDEN LEVEL PLAN

SERVANT

SEAT   FIREPLACE

DESK

STUDY

GARDEN

LOGGIA

DOWN   UP

ENTRY

UP

BEDROOM

SCREEN

BEDROOM

BEDROOM

W

BATH   BATH

D

W

GRASS   BANK

All now in so many new forms are actually aiming against the city, on the side of the original space-loving primitive.

Miracles of technical invention with which our "hit-and-run" culture has had nothing to do are—despite misuse—new forces with which any indigenous culture must reckon.

ONE: Electrification. Given modern electrification, distance is all but annihilated so far as human communications go; and by electric light human occupation continuously illuminated. Radical change in the entire basis of civilization.

TWO: Mechanical mobilization. Given the steamship, airstrip, and automobile, the human sphere of contact immeasurably widens. By the many mechanical modes, by wheel, air or ship, this radical change in the basis of our civilization is taking place.

THREE: Organic architecture: natural building. Given the Principles of nature, material resources become something no longer to be fought against but fought for. Now available to man in the air, sea, or mud under his feet, are the natural bases of human use by good design. With organic architec-

TYPICAL COTTAGE FOR LEVEL GROUND (PREFABRICATION)

ture his resource, man is a noble feature worthy of his own ground; integral there, as trees, streams or the rock ribs that are the hills. Rational changes in our civilization are imperative now because the individual himself, when no longer merely a creature of taste, becomes creative. Architects of the democratic spirit are here, demanding deeper organic foundations for an organic society. Everywhere this new American architecture is demanding more organic foundations for economic, ethical, social, aesthetic daily life; insists all future planning now begin *at the beginning*. Planned revolution by evolution is *now* organic.

The sense of space in spaciousness is not only scientific (it always was) but now fruitful, a genuine becoming. Congested senseless verticality is both inartistic and *unscientific!* To this spiritual awakening of the architect comes the space-loving human being as client. To freedom-loving democracy all stricture is as intolerable as it ought to have been so long ago.

Wherever the welfare of human life is concerned stricture, vertical or horizontal, cannot stand against the more natural conscientious harmony of life with the ground.

TYPICAL HOME FOR SLOPING GROUND

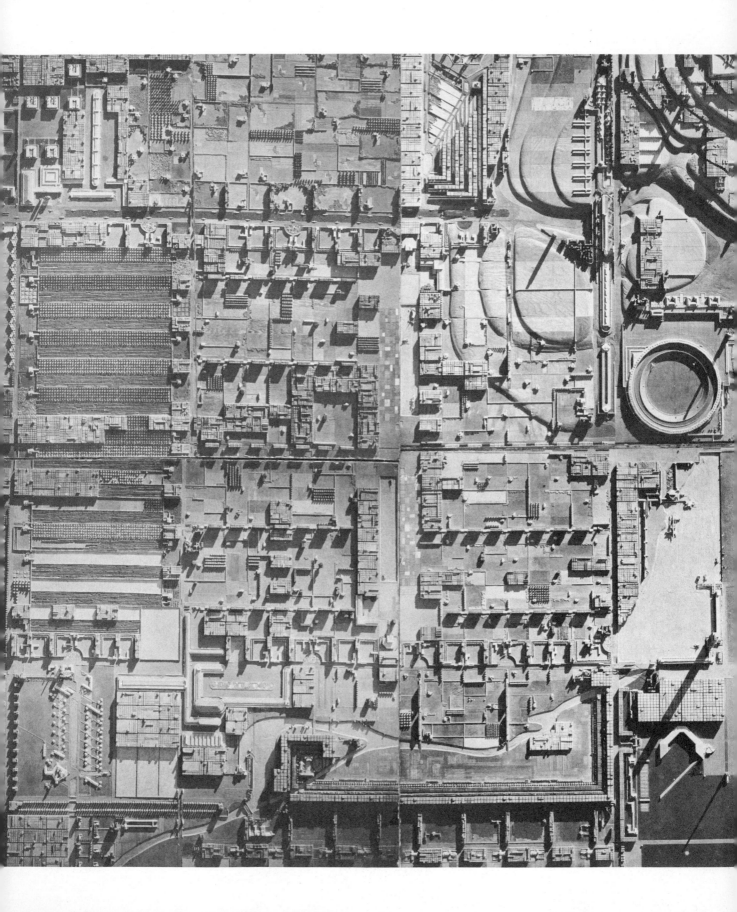

Another greater force to aid the reawakening instincts of the ancient adventurer lies in the spiritual strength of this challenge as a superb ideal of human freedom: Democracy! This new-old ideal is ancient as a spiritual concept of life, but is new to our own phase of modern time. See its natural consequence as the reintegration of Decentralization! With this new spiritual concept, we move beyond prevailing expedients. Organic architecture is integral; a concept of this new life our nation *is* learning to identify as free democracy. Yet only dimly comprehending this new-ancient ideal, architecture, because itself inevitable to all appropriate forms of civilization, must become a great spiritual force moving to free mankind from time-bound life in time-bound modern cities. Decentralization is therefore innate necessity: a new city is inevitable as sunrise tomorrow morning though rain may fall.

Thus the three principal machine agencies are steadily at work for the surviving instincts of the freedom-loving primitive. Democracy steadily approaches. And while yet unconscious of the precise forms it will take, we are able to see new forces gathering.

Look again and again at these modern machine agencies, busy forcing change upon this "best of all possible worlds." Examine each—more in detail. Then study the basic ideals of this young-old champion of Freedom, already at work around the world: Organic architecture—and you will begin to understand Broadacre City.

Looking Backward

Earlier in time human intercommunication could only be had by direct personal contact. Commercial or social communication was slow and difficult. The City was of necessity a close-built mass—a mart, the only general meeting place, therefore the only distribution center. So the pattern of the feudal city grew to serve human needs as they then were. Human concentration, then, was not an unmixed evil. Such cities as there were grew as organisms; grew naturally as the organism of our own body grows; the natural result of proper feeding. Acceleration of tissue by circulation and chemical activity such as characterizes a malignant tumor did not then

67

manifest itself. The city then was not malignant. The ancient city was not opposed to the course of normal human life in relation to natural beauty of environment; it was as inevitable as it was desirable. Cities of ancient civilizations grew to relieve pressures then caused by the lack of the integration now possible to us. Those ancient civilizations have perished.

Perhaps learning lessons from the past, modern European cities wisely resisted skyscrapering and remained nearer human scale. But our own survivals of these ancient cities have gone on absorbing from the countrysides what they could never repay; exaggerating the productions of industrialism at expense to agriculture. Ignorant of the culture which agronomy should have meant to our country, we chose to follow the British line of industrialization.

But not one of our big cities can subsist long on its own birth rate as birthright; therefore, a vampire, it must renew itself from our farms and villages.

Feverish excitations of the industrial urban ganglia (owing to pressures caused by fundamental changes such as we are describing), have grown abnormal, therefore painful. Concentrations of about two hundred or more persons to the acre are often considered "practical" (see London, New York or Tokyo) in planning or replanning cities.

Gather so many people together, visible on every acre, and try to imagine freedom and the pursuit of happiness left to each in housing them by the square mile!

Any wise recognition and definition of freedom under Democracy must say that ultimate human satisfactions no longer depend upon but are destroyed by density of population.

Our new machine agencies create new tendencies consciously employed; or deployed and reorganized. Civilization recapitulates. The village that became a city scatters far, as mobilized communication grows: agency number one. There is now no advantage in a few blocks apart, over a mile or two or even ten. There is a new time-scale to take the place of the old foot-and-inch scale. Human thought itself long since rendered ubiquitous by printing, now by visible speech and movement, all but volatile: telegraph, telephone, radio, television and safe flight. Then what have we? But the proper question is, what has us?

Concerning agency number two: steam, once upon a time dependent on fuel concentrations, congested and coupled close together human devices for movement and living comforts. But the internal-combustion engine (motor car or plane) safely goes anywhere carrying its own fuel, smoothly working as it goes. The motor ship, the automobile, and the airplane. Transit through space becomes economical. New hard roads or rails still come in, because of still necessary composition with these advantages. Developed as continuous avenues of swift, fluid mass communication, these are all comparatively new devices, breeding still more devices and advantages.

Results of agency number two are countless mechanical systems of ventilation, refrigeration, heating, and lighting, making dependence upon the centralized service-systems of the old city superfluous.

Agency three: new materials, fibrous steel—the spider spinning—used in tension, high-pressure concrete in compression, glass and innumerable plastics. Broad, thin, cheap sheets of plywood, sheet metal, or cement which together with sheets of similar insulating value make completely new types of building design admirable. Buildings may be so economized by intelligent standardizing that "home" may now be open to beautiful environment and be designed to broaden the life of the individual family, making site and building a unit.

Tendency number four: inorganic prefabrication: degeneration of quality by mass production. While utilities are made better and cheaper, new designs are needed to be made available for all, instead of more and questionable luxuries for the few. Machine design is now principal means of making use of power for decentralizing the big city and dispersing it; collecting it into what we, at first, call the countryside (not meaning suburbs); but, uniting desirable features of the city with the freedom of the ground in a natural happy union: such reintegration as here called Broadacre City. A city of native creative ability, its advantages, we hope to see, turning the capabilities of the machine spread *for* the human being not

69

THE USONIAN CONCRETE BLOCK HOUSE

USONIAN HOUSE LIVING ROOM

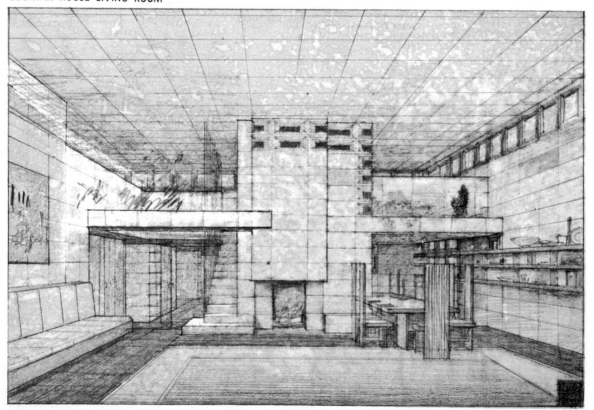

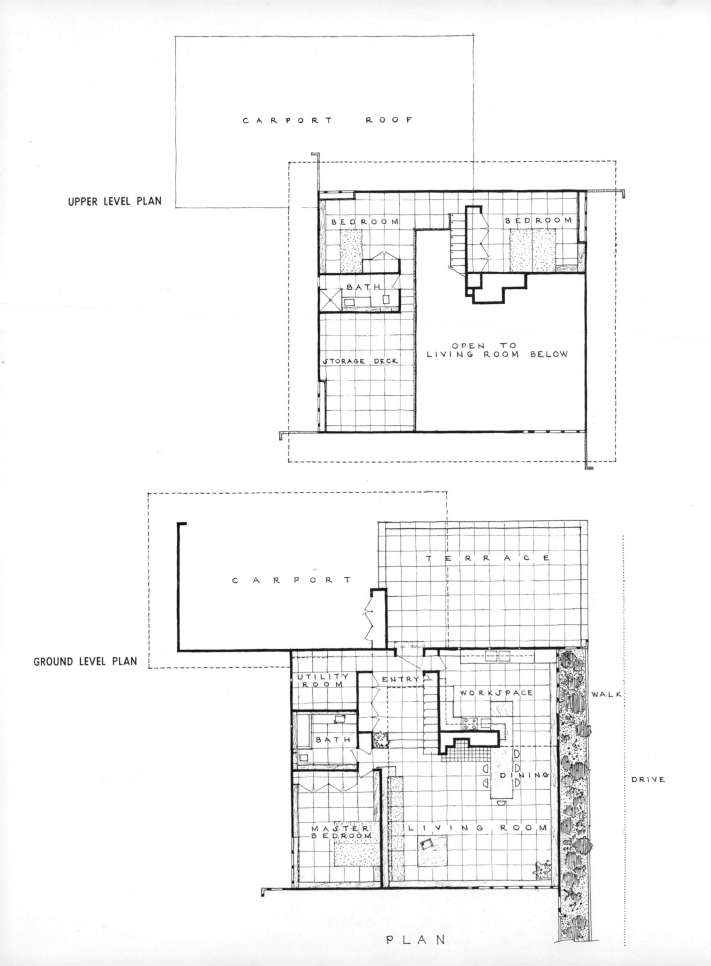

CARPORT ROOF

UPPER LEVEL PLAN

BEDROOM

BEDROOM

BATH

STORAGE DECK

OPEN TO
LIVING ROOM BELOW

CARPORT

TERRACE

GROUND LEVEL PLAN

WALK

UTILITY
ROOM

ENTRY

WORKSPACE

BATH

DINING

DRIVE

MASTER
BEDROOM

LIVING ROOM

PLAN

stacked against him. We have earned good right to speak of this city of tomorrow, the city of Democracy, indulging in no double-talk, as the City of Broad Acres.

Freedom—or Conscription

Individuals are still capable of developing selfhood instead of selfishness (consciously or unconsciously) and we go first to this free, more democratic individual, as the individual we must work with for the right human uses of the machine. By this time the machine is not only a runaway but revolutionary; and reactionary to such human values as the industrial-revolution has allowed to live. The runaway, imperceptibly at first, forcing the old city into new forms. The more intelligent citizens now lead the way to freedom for others. Numbers, increasing, come trailing along into that spaciousness we will soon have *good reason* to call the freedom of American democracy.

Character is a healthy individual growth of freedom from within. No matter how the present pilots of our civilization came to be pilots, unless the people themselves want to go down to stay down, they must act upon the modern imitations of ancient feudal cities inimical to our new means of life. They must act upon them not as calamity but as opportunity for development of the *quality* now belonging by nature to them throughout every feature of their daily lives.

Decenter and reintegrate. When this need is seen as indispensable, democracy will be built. Only the spirit of an energetic freedom-loving people disciplined from within by means of true nature-study; employing natural methods and whatever materials art, organic architecture, science (and religion) have in common; using our new advantages; only such *command* will ever know indestructible power—unbreakable defense. Of such should be the character of these United States. Say, Usonia? Aristocracy from within, which our forefathers hoped to see a reality—interpreted by Thomas Jefferson as "the bravest and the best."

Why then should free men not use the power of machine leverage to gain and keep the freedom their own forefathers declared?

Individuality independent—the Sovereignty of which we have already enough unselfish manifestation to live and grow the new city by—is continuing to make the old city increasingly unimportant—even as a burrow. Driven to sky-hooks, nooks and crevices—inhibition everywhere—the big-city now can exist only to be thwarted or aborted.

"Full employment" as we continually hear about it is not enough for the democratic citizen if this country still means what it declared—1776. No. "Full employment" is not enough because it may be and often is only a more subtle form of rent or conscription continued as the useful means centralization now holds out. It is the baited hook to keep the worker dangling.

No human soul, healthy, grows or even long survives sterilizing practices of the vicarious machine life as are common to this machine age. Urban life—à la mode—can be little more than some kind of surrender to the all-devouring god: Expediency. As petty social and official exactions increase, always the underlying purpose is found in some form of rent. You can call rent, too, a form of conscription. The modern crime of crimes against Democracy is conscription in any form, because conscription is inevitably a form of *confiscation*. Conscription is the form of rent most hateful to democracy because it soonest destroys freedom at its very source.

Our soul grows more by what we give than by what we take and feed upon. No man's soul grows by what is exacted from it. When he signs away his sovereignty as an individual he is not far away from the lowest form of socialism the world has ever seen.

PART THREE

DECENTRALIZATION

Integration on the New Scale of Spacing

OUR share in the Americas—why not call that share Usonia?*—can no longer be earned without good architects as essential interpreters of America's humanity. Creative architects. Nor can this nation afford to believe creative architecture is not to be its own logical interpretation of ways and means of life in our modern machine-made era. Art, Philosophy, Economics, and Religion, all old-school, have failed us, and politics is becoming likely as prostitute in a drift toward conformity. Organic architecture now comes as natural interpreter of Nature. It should light the way? Any true creative art can know the way. After our long journey—at least 500 years long—away from the original art of Architecture the mother-art, other arts, though not so integral with the daily life of the human being, now show signs of awakening. But in fundamental social affairs of Form (not *re*form) the architect is necessarily our prophetic interpreter in such circumstances as are common to our fate. The new forms will be provided by him. The nature of the true architect-mind is most needful now as in any era of Change. Great ancient powers that built great civilizations (abstractions) only to die, still live on in us to help build a civilization able to survive the fate that overtook them. We do know that ancient cities, however they were conquered or destroyed by force, have perished because of external ideals of life—life from outside in—not life from inside out.

------

* Samuel Butler's suggestion of a name for our nameless nation (see his *Erewhon*).

We know, too, that the same old human power they died of, and with, is infinitely multiplied in our case by enormous mechanical exaggerations. But were we so to use machine power as to build new freedom for man, *free in the organic city* now inevitable to our civilization, we might live indefinitely! Why then more temporizing with all the *external* ideals which have proven fatal?

It is nearly two thousand years since the assertion of the organic truth that "the kingdom of God is within *you*." This new dynamic interior ideal we are calling democracy has grown up gradually in the human heart. But we of these United States have neglected to build a life—therefore a city—natural to us. A natural architecture of a natural economic order of the natural state. Organic.

An experiment? Yes, and if by "experience" it succeeds, and this union we are calling Usonia turns from the present static to the integration of decentralization inevitable to our ideal of democratic life, only then will we turn toward the new freedom: laws made for man not man made for laws. Integral livelihood for the citizen, artist and all laborers in the vineyard. And for all artisans a life based squarely with good sense upon good ground.

Coming now to the individual "at home": he will be organically related to landscape, to transport and distribution of goods, to educational entertainment and all cultural opportunity. All as easily imagined now. But the individual home democracy will build is in itself new freedom and freshness from within which other civilizations have only partially attained.

This ideal of the Usonian home is where organic architecture first comes in to meet rising demands for integrity of means with social ends, by radical change in *basic structure:* one great fundamental improvement brought into the service of the American citizen *as individual.*

First decentralization, then planned reintegration. Reinterpretation of our life by modern art and science will soon point the way forward to this realization. So work, leisure and culture; Art, Religion and Science; all will be, nearly as possible, *one.* Only then may each man be a whole man, living a full life. Only then is he "secure." Nor does that mean that every man must be a genius or farmer. But there will be no longer excuse for any man to be the kind of parasite the machine power of centralization is now so busy making of him—only to ensure him "employment" on the terms of a wage-slave?

78

We now know that these new machine forces may be potential, great liberators, but we know they are yet far from working so for the citizen. They are not owned by him nor are they owned for him. They are owned by the same landlords, machine-lords, and money-lords that operate rent and operate the city, itself now a vicious form of rent. These misdirected mechanical means are potential means of human liberation. But thus warped to distortion, enormity is maintained to destroy the citizen.

It is within the power of these very mechanical forces to automatically destroy any system that continues to deprive humanity of all but a small fragment of its potential benefits.

As a people we are still unfamiliar with the idea, but it is organic character in planning and building that alone can lead the way out of this terrific collision of mechanical forces. Organic architecture can end this superwaste of human life, now become so commonplace that we thoughtlessly accept its evil consequences as inevitable. Normal though not inevitable, it may become fatal to our national experiment in freedom.

In this city of today, as of yesterday, ground-space is reckoned by the square foot. In the organic city of tomorrow ground-space will be reckoned by the acre. No less than an acre to each individual man, woman and child. This individual acre seems minimum when we consider that if all inhabitants of the world were to stand upright together, they would scarcely occupy the island of Bermuda. Reflect that in the United States there are about fifty-seven green acres each for every man, woman and child within our borders at this time.

On this basis of an acre to each, architecture could soon come into service of the man himself as a natural feature of his life. The architecture of his home could never again be the adapted, commercialized thing it is: as housing by government or otherwise. Overcrowding itself to be sold; sold again. Resold. Overcrowding oversold life by taxi-meter: the realtors standing by to "see to it" that there be no more standing room than lively competition demands and he feels he can afford. Artificial scarcity thus chronic in any form is no boon now.

Liberal ground use is itself now one sure basis for culture and a more liberal education for America.

As our society learns to see life as free and believes man to be trusted, the citizen will learn to see architecture as the essential expression, the true protection natural to freedom; because good building is itself a form of organic life. Be sure that the ultimate Usonian City will thus be on its own foundations, and be its own impregnable defense.

Imitative eclecticisms now so widely practiced, however tastefully so-phisticated, are only some bad form of crooked sentimentality. Personal "taste" can seldom be more than superficial because it is merely selective: some sentimental exploitation of something or other from somewhere that someone else approved—somehow. As we now practise what society is pleased to call "taste," taste is a kind of knavery. The jackdaw, the magpie, the cuckoo, the monkey—all "eclectics" by nature! But why man? It is more than merely unfortunate that our experiment in the birth of a nation has really known the creative artist only on such terms. The imitator never actually learns. His "conversion," when it occurs, is merely a turnabout to some other form of eclecticism. This man may know all about everything and understand nothing. Expediency is eclectic as eclecticism is taste expe-dient forever.

Taste peripatetic tried long ago to pick and choose the external effects that might lead, instead of letting life lead as native and so teach man constructively how to work and live. Natural. So man himself has become little more than a palliative, the quality of his luxury spurious. At his best overeducated, "best" is likely to be very worst. The huckster you hear on the radio; the star you see in the movies; the designer whose work is on manufacturer's lists; hopeless deterioration by way of taste. As a conse-quence, see what "sells."

If the true architect's faith still lives, it must live as it has always lived: as honest experiment made by courageous, intelligent radicals in love with the poetic principle—and practicing these principles as architecture.

Only the faith that keeps radical faith with life itself is fit to be called safe! This is as true wherever great political co-ordination is effected as it is where good building is done. But no worthy experiment founded on expe-rience is the same thing as one merely experimental.

Let us now approach the growing traffic or any other pressing city problems as another *human* problem; not as tinkers trying to tear parts of the city down only to build it up again on its old site while declaring that "architecture has nothing to do with humanity"—the approach that is exactly what has made the difficulty.

We have plenty of occasion to know that vested interests cannot be divested by agreement; but, unless by force, only by sincere educational revolution. "Interests" will never voluntarily agree to the loss of their immediate quarry which lies in some form of rent. Perhaps even rent for rent.

Observe for another page or two this inner law of organic change now at work upon these big, bigger and biggest cities. Inexorable Law of Change! Law with inevitable drastic consequences. First and forthcoming consequence the organic city of this discourse: the city of the new freedom, Broadacres.

Broadacres

Nonsense is talked by our big skyscraperites in the blind alley they have set up, defending urban congestion by obscuring the simple facts of the issue. Of what use, in modern light, is the surgery of these superspacemakers for rent—professional promoters of the congestion-promoting traffic problem? Their skyscraper-by-skyscraper is the dead wall of our obstruction, the gravestone of capitalistic centralization.

For similar reasons the traffic problem (as we call our danger, our distress and eventual disgrace), if tied up with the skyscraper, is insoluble by any busy big city in the United States or elsewhere.

But the door of the urban cage is about to open.

The amorphous herds of humanity swarming in the narrow, erstwhile village lanes and caverns may now take wings as well as go on wheels. All increased speed facilities of movement are lateral. All, in point of time, are comparative flight.

In the new time scale the door of the urban cage is surely opening wide. Motorcar invasion and collateral inventions in the air and on the rails are leading up to total mechanization of transit.

So not only is the actual horizon of the individual immeasurably widened but his entire range of life (why not thought?) is broadened on the ground by these mechanizations when properly put to work. It is significant that not only have *space* values entirely changed to *time* values, now ready to form new standards of movement-measurement, but a new sense of spacing based upon speed is here. Mobility is at work upon man in spite of himself. And, too, the impact of this new sense of space has already engendered fresh spiritual as well as physical values. A ride high up in the air, in any plane or elevator, only shows man how fast and far he can go away on the ground. It is this broadened view that inspires in modern man his desire to go. If he has means, he goes. He has the means in his motorcar, copter or plane. And the horizon keeps widening conveniently for him as he goes.

Observe this physical release at work upon the citizen's character as a spiritual thing—an inspiration as well as new satisfaction and implement.

When the citizen realizes this release, his selfish interests may still pull away and pig-pile him senselessly in high tiers of cells upended on hard pavements. Dazed by his new freedom, he may be like some animal born in captivity; but when he finds the door of his cage open, he will soon learn like the animal that he can go free. When he learns that he is free, he is gone perhaps only to come back by habit—for a time.

After all is said and done, *he*—the citizen—is really the city? The city is going where he goes. He is learning to go where he enjoys all the city ever gave him, plus freedom, security and beauty of his birthright, the good ground. The first true basis for his pursuit of happiness is such integral independence: the only sure basis of his desired freedom.

Throughout our amazing civilization the citizen is already going "afield" because the machine that brought him to the city is as able to take him back again. When he wakes to a larger and better sense of himself he is free to go out and—prophetic—build the new city. Machine power *subjected* to man's own proper use will enable him as a citizen to live in a better city in a better developed countryside because he is no longer conscript either by or for the agencies now keeping him at least available as one.

Democracy on these new free terms means freedom for every citizen— yes, but only if the principle of the machine is forced *by himself* to go to work *for* him. It could start working *for* him if he should so desire and courageously so decide. The machine as an automaton is involuntary. Automatically (because of what it really is), the present uses of it work

82

man toward the revolution which this decision may mean. Otherwise this great iron horse upon which the West rode to power—the industrial revolution—is not only a runaway horse but a stayaway.

To repeat: as centralization was the natural "monarchy" (in architecture the major axis and minor axis), men were compelled to centralize and revolve as closely as possible around an exalted common center, for any desirable exploitation of the man-unit. The idea of democracy is contrary. Decentralization—reintegrated—is the reflex: many free units developing strength as they learn to function and grow together in adequate space, mutual freedom a reality.

Analysis

Consider: monarchy was defeated because it magnified, while at the same time it deliberately mortified, the individuality that we, as a people, desired and declared; and now, I believe, desire more than ever to establish? As for our present system, free enterprise, so called: well, if its beneficiaries should decide to persist in the present form of supercentralization, the system—its apex on the ground, base in the air—now stands ready to fall. It will fall for the same reason that masonry falls or monarchy falls, as all despotism surely falls: the law of gravitation and the law of diminishing returns (a law of nature).

The mechanized forces now employed in the building of our mad world are turning upon the remaining peak of monarchic despotism now demoralized: the now overgrown old city. Do the hurrying fools blindly driving production to still further excess in big cities still imagine they are building the city up? But all nature is against them. They are tearing the city down.

Centralization is centripetal, whether as city, factory, school or farm; it has not met the rising spirit of democracy—freedom of the individual as individual to work with—for centralization is by nature against it. Many obvious details (traffic problem for one), also have enormous powers now setting in dead against the principle of centralization. Machine power itself now denies centralization in spite of its ancient masters, because it is in the nature of intercommunication and ubiquitous mobility that the big city decenter itself and spread out far away—spread thin, growing high and higher only as it goes outward from center. The countryside is the place for the skyscraper. If higher at all, then wider on the ground. It is in the nature of the development of flying, too, that the present city disappear eventually to reappear as well spaced structure in spaciousness. The old capitalistic city is no longer safe. It is mass murder. Even though no bombs ever appear as murderer. The true humane city is Broadacres.

By way of unnatural survival of the big citified city, capitalist centralization has had a bold day but can have no relatively long day. It is easy to see now that though not dead yet, what it really is is neither necessity nor luxury but harmful stricture, wasting humanity. So our big cities, vampires, must die. Universal automobilization, ubiquity of movement, thought, voice and vision now penetrating distance and walls—these are gigantic factors making present-day urban life as troublesome to free human life as static is to radio.

What about the time when these rapidly increasing "modernizations" become universal? Time not far away.

Democracy by Definition

Already men get more satisfaction out of their vastly increased facility for free movement than ever before. Imagine a man's life in the next twenty-five years, if man can keep out of industrial war long enough to get enough out of the last war to let the machine do its work for his own democracy?

Democracy: the integrated society of small units each of the highest quality imaginable and all characteristic. Genuine. This is in the nature of our rational ideal of the free world, and practical too, but only so if this machine age be taken well in hand not only by science but by organic character in art and architecture—in statesmanship as well—and effectively used in the nature of all materials according to intrinsic nature. Exaggerated artificialities of educational enterprises today—skyscraper the urban devil—have already gone far out of human scale. The humane and smaller unit made free and effective upon the whole surface of the nation everywhere is on its way. This is democratic. Salvation of the civilization we really do desire is in this free life of honest democracy. I believe we are now able and willing to pay the price for such growth as it presents.

Then let us have done with all exaggerated vertical lanes of elevator traffic in the rank and file: vertical transport impinging upon congested narrow lanes below—all channels crowding in upon these narrow closures called "courts"—all cutting in upon desirable privacy. Why make more concessions to makeshifts "authorized" by makeshift rules and regulations? No more submission to crucial (and cruel) landlord expedients. We know now that crowding is a ruse and has no beneficent solution except to inspire us to plan the new city.

Land and Money

What the nation has been calling democracy is really only mediocrity rising into high places—mobocracy. Let us now look at human life in America through native and natural eyes, yearning for a society safe from the license of the mobocracy which is taking the place of conscience.

Common realty achieved by way of taxation on communal resources, as Henry George pointed out with complete logic, is entirely democratic. But his "single tax" was only an expedient and never intended to be taken as a complete solution of our land problem. Serving its purpose: when economic liberation of land and money is duly effective, none may say how far man's cultural liberation may go with greater aesthetic uses of his ground by way of the vast mechanical resources developed in the past century. By proper organic use of our new materials, steel, concrete and glass, if developed in the new spirit of organic architecture, our nation will build with a beauty monarchy and empire hardly dreamed.

Interior discipline of trained imagination is needed for good citizenship, and needed to adapt modern machine craft to such higher uses as would expand and enrich the quality of all human life. This, too, is a matter of good natural architecture.

But first of all we need a new aesthetic—also a new idea of what consti-

85

tutes "profit"; a new idea of what constitutes Success; a new idea of what constitutes luxury. Beauty in all its phases as a native must grow naturally among us here. Else no life is worthy life. Machine power, decentralized and better distributed, more directly and simply applied to humane purposes, is the clear basis of any practical expression of social life here in this twentieth century. Developed machine-age life, as luxury, must consist in more appropriate use and intelligent limitation of machinery in devising new patterns inevitable for life in the New. Then will come a universal margin of leisure, greater rational freedom for the individual than any known by previous civilizations—but this only if the creative artist is there in his true place; the machine in his hand as a tool.

Why, then, should we try so hard to make life and buildings look hard, like machines? Why breed a tough mechanized citizenry, merchants commercialized by machinery? Why insist upon a merchant-motive, confusing romance with sentimentality, destroying both? Though modern buildings may have the clean lines and surfaces of a well-balanced machine, that is only the bare basis for beauty affirmative. But when they are merely negative? However novel at the moment, negative is only tentative. Power directly applied to purpose, with the inspiration of genius, is the basis for all good building or good life. But the spirit of man desires more because man's spirit *is* infinitely more—a nobility and exuberance.

It is not much to have discovered that a single mechanical unit may be infinitely repeated by machinery in construction or that it may be a great economy. (Though it may not be.) It is far more important that an infinite variety of appropriate forms and schemes may result when machine powers are placed in heads and hands guided by the creative instinct: the imagination of a mind with a humane heart aware of the grace and significance of beauty.

Organic Architecture

Organic architecture has demonstrated the fact that severe machine-standardization need be no bar to even greater freedom of self-expression than ever known before. If by "self-expression" we mean fruits of genuine individuality and do not mean a sterile style—the cliché—or idiosyncratic taste. All casual discoveries are not necessarily the Magna Charta of the new liberty into which the architect—by interior discipline—may go by way of the machine to teach his own people not foolishly to *re*build but to build the new beyond the old; to build a nation that is itself more like one great organic life altogether; to show now how to go forward into organic life universal. Served by machinery, yes, but only to humane extent and purpose. By this new means the artifex himself goes forward to build buildings far more natural to life for the more natural men and women of this more natural city than the Western world has known: this is organic architecture and this is Broadacre City.

Unknown to most of our citizens, this more natural city is already, by native circumstances, being forced upon us all. This city is happening now upon the very ground whereon we stand; forced by circumstances we fail to recognize as advance agents of decentralization. These agents are becoming so commonplace in our view that we fail to apprehend them.

Then why not be intelligently directed by the inevitable—our lives qualified, by learning prophetic command of organic design?

Only shortsighted interests that continue to overbuild our cities would deny that these nineteenth-century survivals of our own Imitation-renaissance have become too costly. Wherever distribution and transport are concerned, they are a much too serious handicap on production and a terrible imposition upon all parents and children in any aspiring family life. In democracy the family is norm. The family holds within itself the very seeds of culture that is native, organic therefore, and has a future. Organic architecture, this architecture of the twentieth century, is more than half a century past due in our cities.

Senseless waste of time and energy like the wasteful back-and-forth haul due to the skyscraper is symptomatic not of urban success but of excess. Failure. Make good ground free, available to good men for humane uses. As for the poor, subsidize traffic to the country, modify terms of ownership so that every man may have incentive to work and learn to make good use of men's tools on fair terms. All that is necessary for the new city of decentralization to spread wide, grow strong, the citizen free. Otherwise no city will grow strong or free, and we are doomed to a life more and more vicarious and deformed.

What, then, is the basic thought here working for the organic change now essential to growth for the man, woman and child—the family—of Democracy?

Action

Well . . . certainly not the same old thought that makes our big cities a landlord's ruse—the further triumph of ignorance over impotence.

Certainly not this current of exaggeration of Old World survivals that impoverish many a free agrarian area, as though every citizen were a mere "collector"—and make unhappy people by turning good ground into a sterile cinder heap. Exaggeration of artificiality now offers specious "relief" by government "spending."

No, not that. Nor the same old survival of thought that turned America's youth into white-collarites and sent them out of agronomy into the city in search of a job—a "job" where at least one hand might be kept in the pocket, a cigarette hanging from the lip, foot on the bar rail.

Not the same old survival of thought that made out of an Old World economic system this legalized "strong arm" economic system of our new world: an arm that must weaken periodically; come down for a "rest" while all the renting and the rented and residue from rent gravitate toward starvation in the midst of plenty. By nature, such "economy" as ours must end in periodic national catastrophe. Depressions. The war a clearing house needed to revive in order to survive! War—actual as well as economic.

Nor can we imagine our survivals to be what seems to look to our authorities like freedom won and held by force. Meantime the law makes many more arbitrary laws having no foundation whatever in ethics nor any fair basis for our economic structure nor any social structure at all in nature. Now—is not the idea of "freedom by force" anachronism? Unthinkable senseless reiterations by our political promise-merchants of falsehoods we hear and see; and the drift again toward the same old impending cataclysm. Our own nation may reach death by way of these many obstinate centralizations of which in some form, civilizations, hitherto in similar agony, have died? Fate can be the result of such force by centralization as we are exercising upon mankind now.

All history plainly shows that "force" did not nor can it ever *organize* the *growth* of anything but resentment, hatred, revenge, more war—the epitome of all ill-will. Anything inorganic never can end fear. War is no less the denial of man's organic life now than it ever was. However expedient we make war seem to be as the clearing house for our fears or our political mistakes in handling our overproduction, restricting distribution by punishing competitors; however afraid, no man of creative conscience—not even a Napoleon—has ever thought of war as other than exorbitant foolish crime and waste. Nor has any truly creative individual ever yet acted upon his own thought otherwise. But war is now machinery and machinery is war when necessary to the machine age economy of our civilization, if present money-trust machinery survives to dominate it in the old name of "self-defense." "Security."

Feudal

Unworthy survivals of feudal thinking have made of our survivals of the medieval city a monstrous conspiracy against the freedom of life. Centralization itself, as a principle, is become only a bad form of rent: an inevitable conscription of mankind. It is the form of conscription which has not only wasted billions, and murdered millions; it has also made of American architecture a bad form of surface decoration. Architecture has become our blind spot. What was offered to the country for the fifth time as a progress fair in 1940 was only the same old Columbian Fair of 1893. Its face had merely been lifted to mark "progress" in 1933. The repeat performance in New York City to call worldwide attention to our "greatness" was really a confession of impotence.

Always the same old thought. Now we see it planted in this era of shopkeeping as the ideal of the prevailing shopkeeper, seated in so many high places of authority. We see it unwittingly fixing higher premiums upon baser qualities. Special privileges in money making or money taking: property holding. Just ahead of the conscript lie fears that have made of the man himself a piece of speculative property by placing these false premiums upon activities characteristic of the wolf, fox or rat in human form.

Thus these Old World survivals will continue to stampede society, standardize the workman himself all in behalf of a vast labor system interlocking with capital. The employer himself is really another piece of property rented. By whom? Employer in the same fix as employee—only higher up. Or else not an employer at all; only groveling survival of the feudal thinking which will eventually break the workman and the employer both together, as one. So employers too are themselves no less the automatic conscript. They, too, are eventually broken on the industrial rent wheel.

No less, the same old struggle for "survival" puts heavy pressures upon the armchairs of universities to deprive American youth of such individual independence of thought and soul as they might otherwise have developed or achieved—turning fresh minds into empty toolboxes by throwing books at their heads while providing no collateral *experience*. American youth a conscript? He is and in so much more than a mere military sense. Conscription has made militocracy inevitable to him in his life. He is educated only by being conditioned, not by being enlightened.

For him survival (always "survival") makes the banker what he has become: a wary, professional acquisitor. The very profit motive he banks with, and upon, puts convenient premiums upon the baser acquisitive instincts as qualities of mankind. Banking heavily on Yesterday the banker is continually stalling, or already betraying, Tomorrow. But he alone among us is not yet a conscript? Why?

In it all we see the same old hangover overhead—fear—immuring men in the same old mantrap, to arrive in the same way—innocuous—at perihelion, impotence. The biggest survivals of the ancient medieval city are now Bedlam. We have been calling them survivals, but really they are monstrous centripetal grindstones grinding man himself to the consistency of whatever else is being machine-made, for sale!

Now all the more true, that machine power can have no meaning except to help make a man instead of a moron or a conscript, and help set him free from all conscription whatsoever—whether military, moral, economic or artistic.

90

"Survival" then in our society simply depends upon rejection of any belief in the thought that conformity to authority plus money can continue to rule the world. And no faith at all in the coward's belief that everything or anything worth a man's time may be made to happen by legal, military or money power. Finally the falsity that native Culture can be no more than some imported complacence, some *external* idea of form. Our national tragedy lies in these confused and confusing survivals of feudal conformities. We have nurtured youth upon this vain idea. This we have done vainly imagining that we were breeding citizens for Democracy. We were not. In fact, we have patterned our chief institutions of "higher" learning upon many an empty inglorious antithesis. From survival to survival again we derive an arrogant substitute for native culture. Now we are applying these substitutes upon the sterile surfaces of our brittle commercial success and trying to force the world to take it from us now on our terms. Or else. Concentrations upon concentered lives within the centralized city, a merciless unceasing gamble. Survival of the big city would leave the people of these United States—Usonia—immured in insignificant, ugly environment, our living unnaturally exaggerated, without joy, with no indigenous beauty created by our vast prosperous nation for itself: goods, goods, goods where grass ought to be—grass where there should be "goods." How then can life be good? Be other than itself "goods"? All life reduced to the level of merchandise—the national art, as a matter of course, salesmanship?

Our Architecture

Call architecture organic to distinguish it from the pseudo-classic order of the schools, derived mainly from grafted attempts at reclassification called the "international style." A cliché.

Architecture is organic only because intrinsic. In the reflex it seeks to *serve* man rather than to become a force trying to rule over him. Another reason why we say organic architecture cultivates "the space within" as a reality instead of the roof and walls: it is building from inside out, instead from outside in. Therefore it is living twentieth century architecture instead of nineteenth century architecture.

This new American concept of architecture has style as the expression of character. No longer is form a question of "styles." Essential Style it has, and is of the nature of all building whatsoever provided only that style be naturally achieved from the nature of the building problem itself and found within the very means for and by which the building stands built. The result: style is character. It is by integration in this interior sense that Broadacre City would give style birth; have great style all the while as something natural; not as something exterior and forced, either in its structure or upon its people. No exterior discipline whatever could rule, nor could *re*classifications be natural. Establishment of flexibility will be the reverse of antique classic externals in American architecture. Architecture and acreage will be seen together as landscape—as was the best antique architecture—and will become more essential to each other. Great architectures will arise within the lifetimes of the civilization actually expressed.

As a people, then, if we understand the eternal principles of Nature, our own especially, and learn to use our riches and industrial machinery upon the vast stores of our new materials to good advantage—use them with faithful sense of fitness to purpose—we will naturally arrive at nature-form with true style. Perhaps (though we need not bother much about that) arrive at what, looked back upon in distance of time, might be Twentieth century, or Usonian, style? Should that come to pass, it would not be so much by any calculated intention as by the fate due to honest production and long-continued practice. Style is a precious, magic circumstance—style is, and always, the death of Style.

Architecture organic, perhaps because first deeply concerned with the integrity of innate structure, first grasped the demand of our modern American life for a higher spiritual order. Perhaps only minds imbued with this deeper sense of structure as natural can perceive the fine integrities of the more livable and gracious human simplicities.

Our enlarged and deeper means of today could now break the strictures upon our life and revive emasculated manhood. If current tools were used even with intelligent self-interest, spaciousness, graciousness and happiness in human life would increase. If intelligent use would back up the enlarged sense of available spacing in modern city life, the citizen would automatically be released and the free city of democracy realized. With appropriate scientific use of the new space-scale to be used now as a time-scale, see the extended highway as one great horizontal line of Usonian freedom expanding life consistently everywhere, not only up and down but lengthwise and crosswise; then you see something of the modern Usonian city approaching—whether you like ir or not—Broadacre City.

See the design of the farm itself (little or big) in true relation to adjoining farms and industry and culture, to you in your villages and all related to our national economy. See sizes and shapes of infinite fields well laid out in good proportion each to each—and man-built occupation of the whole, well adapted to natural contour—tillage itself a charming feature of the landscape; hedgeways, ravines, and waterways themselves proper boundaries. Well, if you can see all this, rhythmic in relation to human use and movement; well-placed buildings related to well-placed roads in suitable places: if you can see "horizontal farming" (contour plowing) properly applied to regions and crops, pastures, animals, related to happy people; if you can see the varied, multiple parts all thus contributing to a great dramatic whole in which you sense the repose of individual human contentment and the exuberance of plenty—the life of the imagination truly aesthetic, in the over-all view from wherever you may happen to stand—then you will get a glimpse of the country-loving life in agronomy of the new Usonian city, belonging by nature to the national agronomy of our democratic future. The agronomic culture of the vast nation our forefathers had some right to expect would come of what they were pleased to call Freedom. Then only will you see Usonia.

You will see the people of Usonian countrysides loving exuberance but hating waste, the waste that is ugliness itself and the ugliness that is itself waste: see a people now suspicious of too easy opportunity to live by the vicarious means being forced upon human behavior by the mechanical imposition interlocking rents, exaggerations utterly empty of beautiful human significance.

The New City

Broadacre buildings would be naturally adapted to the lives of the people who would no longer build or be content to live in prettified boxes or take pleasure in the glassification of a glorified crate however "stylized." Intelligence of life would not allow buildings as ignorant expedients; it would see a bad one as serious impediment to good life. So in the free city now here in Usonian countenance of the countryside, find manhood seeking *organic* simplicity as appropriate *character* in everything; workmen themselves learning to see that organic simplicity is actually the fine countenance of Principle and no less so now in this our machine age than ever it was in ancient times. Rather more so. Yes, and how much more necessary to life are architects themselves who are in love with the poetry of life, they alone could say.

As for growing up in the knowledge of organic architecture: It sees itself as new yet ages old; now a true simplicity by way of simples growing out of the free democratic citizen's own devotion to life on his own ground; the citizen himself something of a farmer there, free of all unfair exactions.

In sunlight universal, see his establishment not as a boxment or burrow in a sterile mass of cars and towers; see him standing free of all such stricture on his own acreage. When the immured citizen realizes this independence, this greater opportunity to live his own life with his growing family, he is already on his way to the life which democracy owes to him and he to democracy. His will to be there is not in spite of but because of himself, himself a potential divinity. Then, is it not his good sense to be able to give such natural direction to otherwise inorganic forces, to go where he finds in the pursuit of happiness the liberty (was it not promised him by national charter?) for a natural, fruitful pursuit?

The architecture of the city may now be basic. Yes. As architecture is basic to essential structure anywhere of the timeless sort we can now build. This is no less the structure of whatever is music, poetry, painting or sculpture—or whatever else man's interior sensibilities may thrive upon when disciplined from within by an ideal. Architecture must see civic life in terms of such human economic freedom as here prophesied; recognize native ground free as the sure basis of a free life in a free city.

94

URBAN SECTION A. VIEW OF CIVIC CENTER WITH NEIGHBORHOOD LAKE AND PARK. ACREAGE FARMS TO THE RIGHT OF THE CENTER. (PHOTOS BROADACRE CITY MODELS: ROY E. PETERSEN)

Teenagers! Wherever building is sensibly modern, or solid walls are vanishing, where dead weight was emphasized by black shadows, super-walls will take their place for you—thanks to you.

Fortifications, that once upon a time protected the might of the baron on his feudal estate, in our day can no longer fortify. As homes, fortifications are dead.

Modern America needs no longer to box up or hole in for protection, or dive into a burrow in any city. Instead security in every sense is best found in the wide free spacing and integral construction, the spiritual perception of what we are calling decentralization. Spaciousness is for safety as well as beauty.

Our vast beautiful country, notwithstanding all the status quo of vested interests is, at perimeter and at heart, gradually becoming more free in spirit as it resents urban constriction. True democratic ideals must—will—go on with this increase of deeper feeling in the popular mind until it reaches the popular heart and makes its feeling for better spacing a universal intelligence. Our vast resources in growing machine power and materials working, in spite of all opposition, to make our ideal actual. What need now for master or slave in any form—however disguised? No need for dictator or conscript. Even if disguised by clever uses of English, we no longer need Lord and Serf. Nor need now for expensive, expanded imitations of ancient feudal masonry by whatever name, no interests vested or divested choosing to call themselves social. Then, for what purpose may our manifold eclecticisms be thought appropriate for such immense vaulting money-power as ours? That tall facade—the "business monument"—already rapidly shifting to somewhere else; or downshore, out of our sight.

When democracy triumphs and builds the great new city, no man will live as a servile or savage animal; holing in or trapped in some cubicle on an upended extension of some narrow street. Withstanding all this passing danger to him—the free man will again live free: the human biped which the best of him always dreamed of being! Life and love as noble leaders of our brave social experiment. Our forefathers declared we would and should so live in spite of commitments to old establishments or property interests or "laws made not for man but as though man was made for laws"; the American living in full consequences of which they could not then foresee.

Usonia

For America today organic architecture interprets (will eventually build) this local embodiment of human freedom. This natural architecture seeks spaciousness, grace and openness; lightness and strength so completely balanced and logical that it is a new integrity bound to scatter servile imitation, to take away all urban stricture and depravity first from the regional field and then—as is the case with all inadvertent health—absorb and regenerate the tissue poisoned by cancerous overgrowth (Urbanism).

Modern gifts—glass, steel in tension, steam, electromagnetic sciences, chemistry, new atomic dissonance, alchemy; these and more, coming or here, implement the new era. We do not recognize their real significance. But we begin to use our own human gifts of creative imagination in the light of organic principles; the poetic principles and ever new ethics of right and wrong according to organic law, these will protect us. We already know that we may hammer heated iron but cannot hammer a stick of dynamite! Wholly new ideas of form will come as clearly to our relief, and joy. So simple and fundamental are the forces which lie beneath, above and within us, as natural agencies of life—that this new freedom is breaking for not against mankind. If the citizen, loyal, will reach out to take these, as they are for what they are—they are his on fair terms.

Facility to roam the sky; from here to there swiftly cover vast stretches of ground; live safely with perfect freedom of communication relating each to all and all in all, his feet on his own ground at will—his life his own when he so pleases, and all the time in his heart what love of home life and country that should mean to a man of free will. All this is not only possible but probable now to the citizen of our country if only he will have the faith in himself to go forward with courage to realize all.

Where, then, is the Usonian citizen situated economically, if he is thus born spiritually?

URBAN SECTION D. A ROADSIDE MARKET. TEXTURED BLOCK MASSES INDICATE FOREST AREAS HELD IN TRUST FOR FUTURE GENERATIONS. TREE-CROPS TO BE SHARED BY THE COMMUNITY. LAND THUS RESERVED TO GO INTO CULTIVATION AS REQUIRED BY GROWTH OF THE POPULATION.

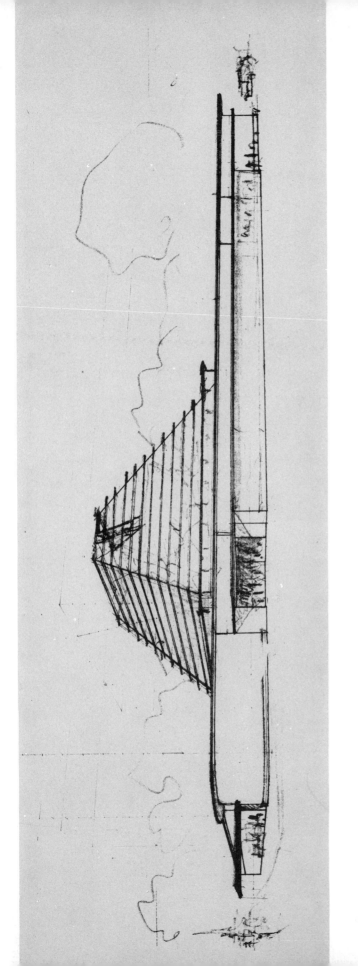

SKETCH FOR ROADSIDE MARKET. "GREAT SPACIOUS ROADSIDE PLEASURE PLACES THESE MARKETS, RISING WIDE AND HANDSOME LIKE SOME FLEXIBLE FORM OF PAVILION — DESIGNED AS PLACES OF COOPERATIVE EXCHANGE, NOT ONLY OF COMMODITIES BUT OF CULTURAL FACILITIES. 'BUSINESS' TAKES ON A DIFFERENT CHARACTER: INTEGRATION OF MERCANTILE PRESENTATION AND DISTRIBUTION OF ALL PRODUCE POSSIBLE AND NATURAL TO THE LIVING CITY."

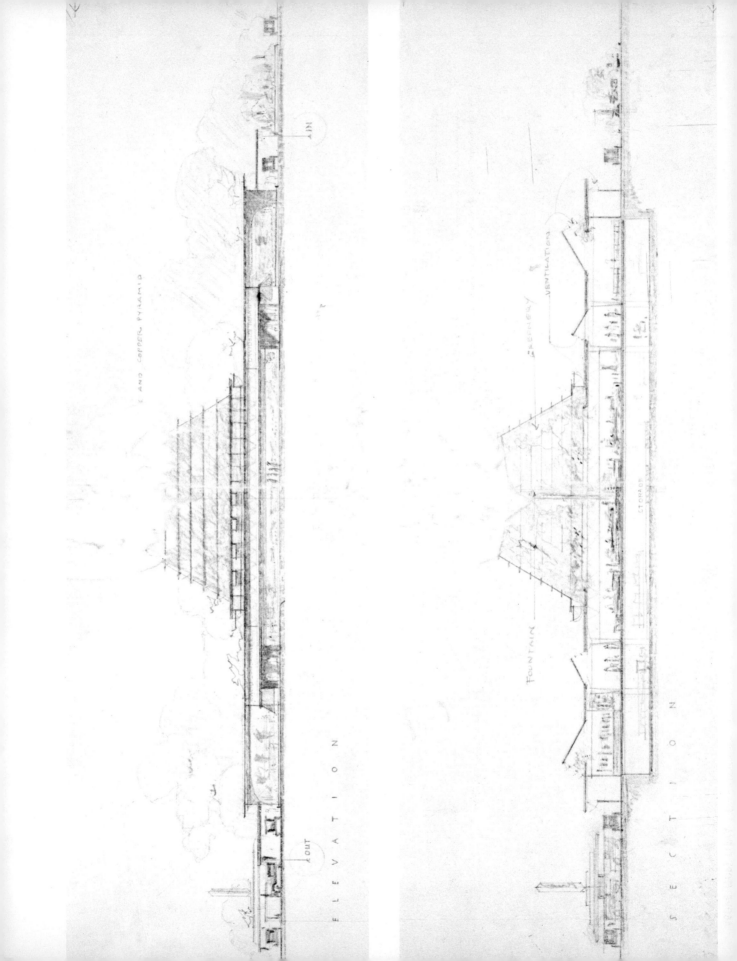

E AND COPPER PYRAMID

E L E V A T I O N

S E C T I O N

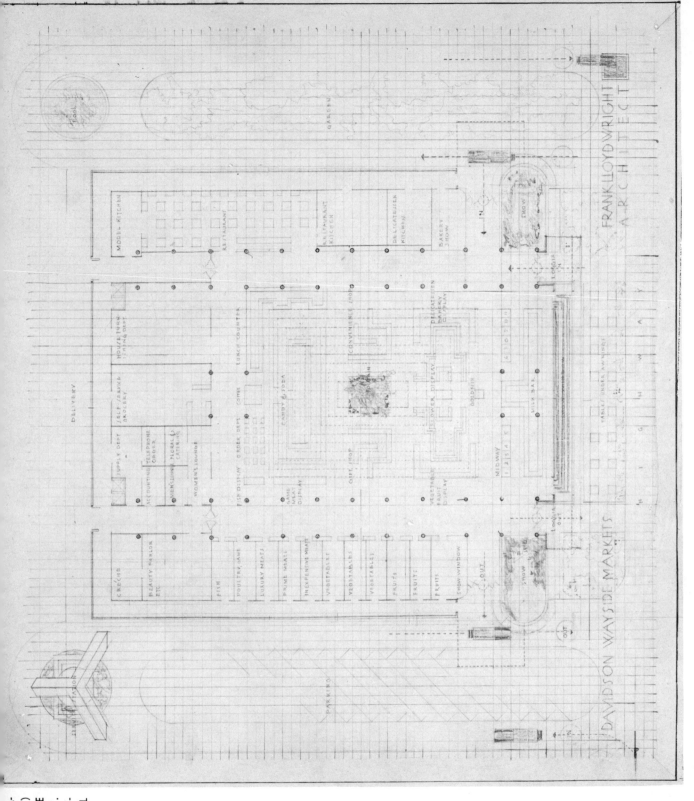

ABOVE (TOP) ELEVA-
TION AND (BELOW IT)
SECTION OF THE
ROADSIDE MARKET.
PLAN AT RIGHT. SKY-
LIGHT OVER CENTRAL
PORTION.

DAVIDSON WAYSIDE MARKETS

FRANK LLOYD WRIGHT
ARCHITECT

Values

Architecture (organic) knows architectural values only as human values, values true not only to Nature but to humanity as nature—or else not valuable! Good or economic modern building is an integration rising to build the organic city—the city that in rising is enemy to all forms of imitation that centralization imposes by impinging upon manhood when free. Neither building nor city is to be there tolerated as any form of *stricture*. Buildings, like people, are sun children, sun-born growth from and with sun-born Nature; and by nature sun-life is life-acceptance in building—or the buildings are not organic buildings. Both buildings and city now should be more truly defense against time, against the elements and the dangerous enemy than the city ever was before.

Architecture may again become true shield for whatever aspiration, glory or sanctity humanity may possess or desire. Organic architecture can be indestructible though machine-made fabric of light fashioned of metals woven into webs of turquoise, green, gold, and silver textiles, or the everlasting hues of the kiln; or cast in metals; or visible in whatever native nature-materials are naturally available, and still be no less integral pattern, the expression of a varied life for free people. If organic architecture is to function for mankind architecture must command every special purpose. Spacious ground must be made available on some fair basis and be legally considered an element having intrinsic value—as free to men as are other elements. Once emancipated by proper zoning and building laws from the tyranny of the exploiters of the "lucky-lot area," absentee landlords, money lords, machine lords (and similar impositions), city building in the new city will stand there free in its own greenery or lie long, flowing lazily and low on the prairie levels, or stretching along the ridges above the ledges of the hills. At one with environment.

Buildings public, private, or industrial, a tall shaft or a streak of light in the countryside enmeshed in metal strands and glass as music is made of notes. What is building without intimate relationship to the ground it stands upon and the inhabitants who occupy it? A great unity, every fine building is necessarily expression of the life it is built to serve directly. So no mere mantraps; no more landlords. No life imprisoned on shelves of vertical

URBAN SECTION B. STADIUM AND CIRCUS FOR COUNTY FAIR AND OTHER PAGEANTRY. MOTEL FOR TRANSIENTS SEEN BEYOND. CIVIC CENTER TO THE UPPER LEFT. SANITARIUM TO THE RIGHT. POLE ANNOUNCING FESTIVALS.

streets above crowds on gridirons down below. No hard faced poster facades.

As life itself builds, so organic architecture builds, no longer allowing man to stumble blindly along the path of the past, unaware as yet of the nature of the malevolent forces that have kept him down, ruining his living present; he seems still unaware of how destructive these modern forces are or in themselves how beneficent they can be. He has started a hell all around him, waiting to damn him now in this new era, to destroy him.

Then why must any status quo of citizenry continue to be some belief, on a par with such "patriotism" (misnamed loyalty) as is "the last refuge of the scoundrel"; or some standardized and sentimentalized academic substitute for culture? No free man can live on outmoded belief continuing too long, some sinister afterglow of feudalism. Again the pioneer takes his place on the frontier. No longer can he of the new order mistake the setting sun of any Renaissance whatever for sunrise.

Must his majesty—the American citizen—go along old-fashioned in his commercial interests, unwittingly in his own image betraying life by reducing all about him to a false, sentimentalized misuse of what was noble in all traditions? Must the common man then, to be common, still insist on practicing petty minor traditions that only turn him wrong end up, maintaining him as some kind of conscript going or coming?

"As loves must die because Love must live," so organic architecture has learned that these too many minor traditions must die in order that the great Tradition we were all born to serve, may live. When we face this, democracy actually comes alive and will plan the new city now already under way with no plan.

Like all principles the principles of organic architecture are simple: the principles of all *entity*: therefore of life itself? No house, nation or system built on makeshift foundations can long stand. So no building built for a life set up on minor or major makeshifts can last long enough. If necessity for such "shifts" be a moral virtue then where lies social weakness?

Good architecture concedes the right to live abundantly in the exuberance of beauty, in the more profound sense in which William Blake defined "exuberance." He did not mean excess nor any form of exaggeration. He meant fullness of the expression of Nature; nor stint nor stunt. That is good architecture for good life.

104

Liberal democratic philosophy yields that primary right to us all. But the only secure foundation we have for any interpretation of life in art, architecture or religion, is *character*. Understanding of Nature as life accepted not merely for fear of the police nor for any merely *expedient* relation between the welfare of the one as against the other, but the wellfaring of the whole. Personal life under democratic government enables one to proceed from generals to particulars. Our youth should be so educated as to discern and stand square with the practical, instead of oblique to the expedient; able to know with sure mind the difference between the mercly Curious and the truly Beautiful.

Now to civilize our architects and cultivate them comes organic architecture. The future awakened civilians of Usonia will be naturally modern; or else all be failures, because Life itself is a changing insistence upon modernity! Life is always modern. Vital forms, fresh, are the continual need to contain or express or prophesy these changes—and do so without waste, sincerely in love with Beauty.

Recapitulation

Once again. *"All fine architectural values are human values, else not valuable."* Humane architectural values are life-giving always, never life-taking.

PART FOUR

URBAN SECTION C. LOOKING OVER LITTLE FARMS IN FOREGROUND TO TRANSPORT LINES AND AIRFIELDS. WAYSIDE MARKETS, FACTORIES TO THE RIGHT.

USONIAN

A Legacy We Have Received From the Past

ARE we all parasites? Whether we like it or not we do work or we do not work. But such bodies as our civilization preys upon if we are parasites seem to be either Nature or the Past? The forces we prey upon and by which we harm ourselves, chiefly, in this machine age are these inevitable forces of Nature. Machine tools have so increased our ability to produce, production has so increased, as to have made riches a kind of poverty; and made truth a kind of anachronism. "Incomes" of rich and poor both added together are an "outgo" that cannot buy the goods we produce at anything like the rate at which the goods, not to say the best, can be produced. So the human labors involved, considered by themselves, unadorned by art, are really less valuable now than ever they were in the past?

Only as idle heirs of civilization, then, are we entitled to a living if we are to be thus displaced by the facilities of machinery! Is it not absurd for man to compete by fertility of mind against the resources engaged in devising labor saving devices for money making schemes as mere gadgetry? The important thing for us all is to so digest these ubiquitous mechanical energies that men may be set free by them for nobler uses, uses more important to the growth of the beauty of life: developments and enjoyments no longer directly concerned with "making money for a living," or acquiring any degree of material power. No man should ever be so bound or time-bound. Nor should any man be a slave to or for "a living." The proper free man should do, in the main, what he really most wants to do when he wants to do, though he may never be able to do all he wants to do of it or for it. *That* really is the only legacy we have received from the past that is valid. Only under democracy genuine can we protect or even understand this legacy.

Individuality

Well, we have been calling this legacy, free from our urban past, "Broadacre City." Broadacres *is* our free city for the Sovereignty-of-the-Individual! Not so simply because it is based upon the minimum spacing of an acre (or several) to the individual, but, more important, because when democracy builds, this is the natural city of freedom in space, of the human reflex. The nature of democracy when actually *built*.

At present, the multiplicity of systems, subversive schemes, especially the 57 varieties in our modern architecture, have gone down so completely as the common expedient as to be too often mistaken by us for civilization itself. Maybe that characteristic, too well practiced, will hang over Usonia indefinitely to postpone any free city of democracy for some generations.

Nevertheless the free city we are considering is squarely within the laws of Change and is already here all around us in the haphazard making, the apparent forces to the contrary notwithstanding. All about us and no plan. Even *in* us—as we now are. The old order is breaking up under the load our senseless weight puts upon us whether we subscribe or do not subscribe.

The capitalism, net, of our nation, is only individualism gone rank or riot, producing either isolationist, authoritarian or unconscientious objectors.

Political partisanship becomes a form of gangsterism. "Party politics" are no true product for nourishment of sentient individuality. Various eclecticisms are the only feature our nation yet knows. The idiosyncrasy of personality resulting not in the individuality needed for democracy but encouraging bureaucracy, and degenerative to mobocracy. Personality, by corruption and consequent degradation of the word "democracy," has got in the way of this great integrity we are calling, as we should, Individuality. In the Jeffersonian sense especially so. But miseducated minds of our day, by mistaking morals for ethics sterilize and standardize instead of fortifying

110

by ethics. By academic training, on account of the resultant à-la-mode political facades, we are everywhere the too willing prey of propaganda by the managed publicity of any "professional." Far too "personal" and credulous as we Americans are, we not only stand in danger of losing our only chance at the free life our charter of liberty held out to us but we are still miscalling this mistake of conformity "democracy," instead of seeing it as and honestly calling it the refined gangsterism of the mediocre or of mobocracy. Democracy is the very gospel of Individuality! Call it what you please. Bureaucratic mobocracy is the corruption that would destroy the fruit of every democratic instinct we have developed.

Specious Authority

Concerning this probable academic attitude of authority itself toward the freedom Broadacres proposes: we have had prohibition because a few fools could not carry their liquor; Russia has communism because a few fools could not carry their power; and now democracy faces a swollen privatism of license instead of true individuality because a few fools could not carry their success! And yet, behind our passion for money-making we must go on making more money to secure more power. If we want power—and we do—we go into the money trust, as we must, or we bust.

Therefore, if instead of the organic architecture of Broadacre City we continue to have a mere styles-formula retained by A.I.A. as architecture, this cataclysm will come because so many mere money-makers have neither the wit, imagination, nor integrity to discriminate between personality the exterior, and individuality the interior; and more capacity for enmity than for gratitude.

By this confusion we continue to overgrow our badly overgrown urban life; and this too because too many capitalist fools pretend to be "conservative." It is their subversive "power" they conserve. This constitutes their own danger as well as ours.

Through adventitious wealth, gained for its own sake by the exploitation of natural resources by machine leverage—the machine now virtually owned by pseudo-capitalism's convenient satellites—the yes-men of our modern, overgrown cities are now an incubus, to be dealt with because they are piling up across the great natural stream of humanity flowing toward economic and spiritual freedom. That "dam" is the first, middle, and, perhaps vain to hope, the last hangover from old feudal systems. Right now, in this very hangover is omnipresent disaster to the freedom of our nation as a great republic true to the principles of democracy.

As I planned the free city, I saw clearly enough a worthy democratic life lying wrong side up before us, if at all. Right side up—in such planning as you may find in the illustrations of these long continued Broadacre studies of freedom—tomorrow: This practical vision of the free city—nationwide—is the city nowhere unless everywhere.

Architecture and Acreage Together Are Landscape

Architectural features of any democratic ground plan for human freedom rise naturally by, and from, topography. This means that buildings would all take on, in endless variety, the nature and character of the ground on which they would stand and, thus inspired, become component parts. Wherever possible all buildings would be integral parts—organic features of the ground—according to place and purpose.

Although present towns and county seats are held as centers, no two districts of the new city need ever be precisely alike. Except as the new city might spread as new feature to some featureless plain. But that plain too, has a certain natural beauty of its own, and might well bear repetitions of the appropriate patterns characteristic of tillage and forestation. Broadacres would be so actually built in sympathy with omnipresent nature that deep feeling for the beauty of terrain would be fundamental in the new city building: would seek beauty of landscape not so much to build *upon*—as to build *with*. Endless unity-in-variety thus becomes a natural consequence. Indigenous character? Inevitable. Endless variety and indigenous character would be the effect of terrain and individuality coming naturally together, wherever they might arise. All would find natural expression, naturally.

Perception and planning, if organic, would be qualified to recognize features of construction and design that would make the physical body of this era of our vast machine age harmonious. Entity. And—to repeat—organic architecture is no less essential to the structure of painting, sculpture, music and religion because, by way of nature, mankind is spiritually awake to the uses and great purposes of all the arts that are all needed to make the culture of a civilization. Inevitably therefore architecture as the great mother-art and moderator contains in principle the essential basis, philosophy, and structure that should inspire them all! Architecture lives again as it has ever lived—*the great final proof of quality in any civilization whatsoever.* Always true basis or cornerstone of a culture.

So, all the way from economic basis to great cultural growth, buildings and good government will be innate features of the free city we have now reached and are about to describe in detail as primarily organic architecture. From great road systems, the natural veins and arteries of the new city, to the various buildings that are its cellular tissue; to parks and gardens that are its pleasure places, its smile; to factories in fields that are its physical subsistence and spiritual health—in the harmony of all this lies the new city of democracy. Primarily, Broadacres would be great architecture.

Were democracy here today in this respect, the entire native scene would soon become harmonious expression of the better nature of modern man himself; would again prophesy and help secure his continuous, happy search for man's growth on his earth. The *native abundance* in which he would then stand and share would be reward for the intelligent use and wise restraint of this gigantic engine of leverage (or of slavery)—the Machine! Our civilization might well be eternal instead of, as now, on the way to join the great rubbish heap of the civilizations which history catalogues, if this true man-light—the Poetic Principle—would dawn afresh for us in such organic character.

The good ground should greatly determine the fundamental shape, even the style, of every occupation in building, road, or institution in the new city. To see where the ground leaves off and the building begins would require careful attention. But this organic "ground-motive," variety in unity, once established in general practice, would be definite and infinite. The ideal of organic unity held firmly in mind, well in hand, the architect would himself gradually become more a spiritual power, equal to his vast new opportunities. Ever growing intelligence of the artifex together with a universal desire on the part of the citizenry for a whole life, all free to grow. This activated, more genuine impulses would soon make at least a work of art of every feature of the new city into which the old one would gradually dissolve. Petty diverse partitions of property, wilful deformations of natural beauty by conscienceless utilities like those of the pole-and-wire men, perpetual defacements by advertising in sordid self-interest becoming common everywhere to irritate the sensitive citizen, would be unpardonable crimes against the landscape. So-called "utilities service" and conscienceless advertising of goods and chattels along the roads by the universal huckster would disappear; mankind going about life in a more normal way; poisonous mechanical gases, groans, shrieks and screams in carbon monoxide gas or smoke—gone. Life itself no longer perpetually endangered by senseless stop and go, jamming, crowding. No more would abortionists be free to set up or set down their glaring paraphernalia by the wayside in attempt to beguile the desired eye. Garish poster facades or signs fighting it out with each other to catch the eye of the helpless passerby, exaggerating everything that can be posted or imagined. Signboards behind which the merchant moves in to live. And much more, not to be that should never have been.

Naturally enough the railroad rights-of-way as may be, belong to the people; and truck lanes occupy the vacant spaces each side along the rails. Operation is another matter. Eventually, the rights-of-way are the most desirable possession of the free city, because, as great traffic truck lanes, they may be turned over to fluid, undated traffic of this kind. Various streams of continuous cross-country traffic, local and long distance bus travel and local trucking should be placed upon these popular railroad rights-of-way, thus restoring the highway to the safe use of the citizen in his automobile.

Like many another established custom now to be liquidated and become proper feature of Usonian Broadacres, these railroad rights-of-way need comparatively little reconstruction except the new type of equipment, inevitable if for no other reason than that the present cumbrous establishment is already obsolescent as human passenger-traffic in America has taken to the air.

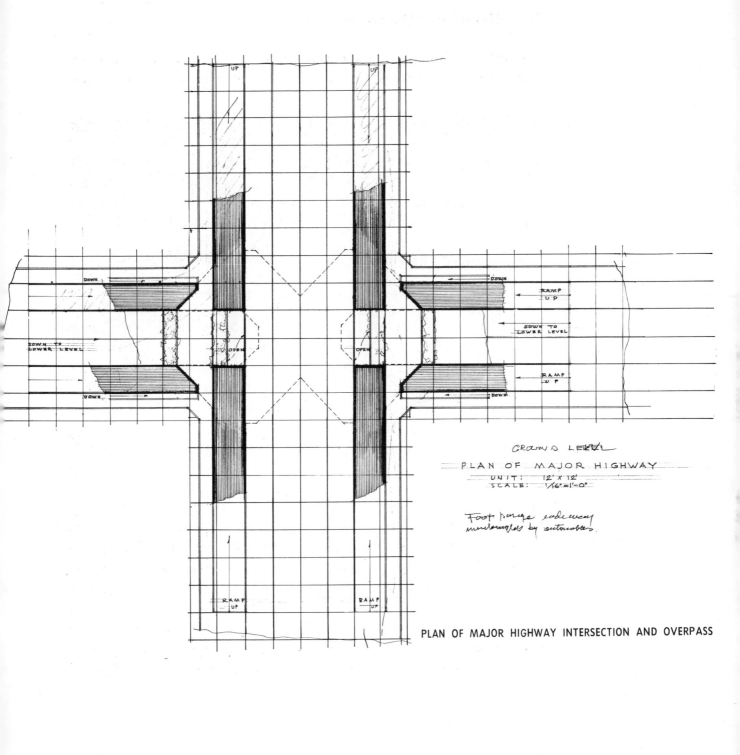

CROWD LEVEL

PLAN OF MAJOR HIGHWAY

UNIT: 12' X 12'
SCALE: 1/16"=1'-0"

Foot passage and ways
unobstructed by automobiles.

PLAN OF MAJOR HIGHWAY INTERSECTION AND OVERPASS

The Usonian Vision

Imagine now, freeways broadened, spacious, well-landscaped highways, grade crossings eliminated by a kind of integrated bypassing, over- or under-

HIGHWAY INTERSECTION MODEL

passing. All traffic in cultivated or living areas made gracious by landscaping, devoid of ugly scaffolding (like telegraph and telephone poles and wires), free of glaring billboards, and especially from ugly fencing and ditching. Imagine these great highways of generous, safe width and always easy grade—roadbeds concave instead of convex—bright with wayside flowers or cool with shade trees, joined at intervals with modern air-rotor fields from which self-contained mechanical units—safe, noiseless transport planes, radio-controlled, carrying neither engines nor fuel—like modern taxicabs take off from convenient stations to almost anywhere else. Giant roads

116

PLAN OF MINOR HIGHWAY

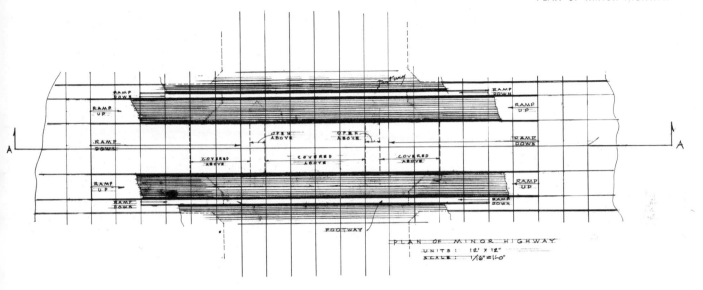

PLAN OF MINOR HIGHWAY
UNITS: 12' X 12"
SCALE: 1/16" = 1'-0"

SECTION OF OVERPASS

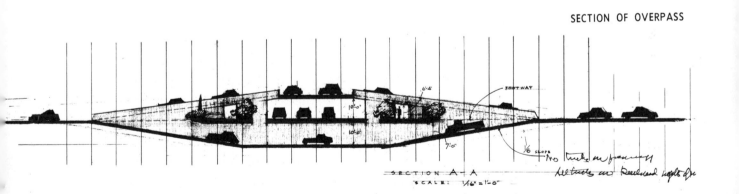

SECTION A-A
SCALE: 1/16" = 1'-0"

OVERHEAD SERVICE STATION

now themselves great architecture. Public service stations now no longer eyesores but expanded as good architecture to include all kinds of merchandise, appear as roadside service along the roads for the traveler. Charm and comfort—no end—throughout these great roads as they unite and separate, separate again and unite. Endless the series of diversified units—as one passes by small farm units, roadside markets, garden-schools, beautiful spacious dwelling places on acreage, each on its own acreage of individually adorned and cultivated ground. Places too for pleasure in work or leisure are common where landscape features occur. And imagine man-units so arranged and integrated that every citizen may choose any form of production, distribution, self-improvement, enjoyment, within the radius of, say,

118

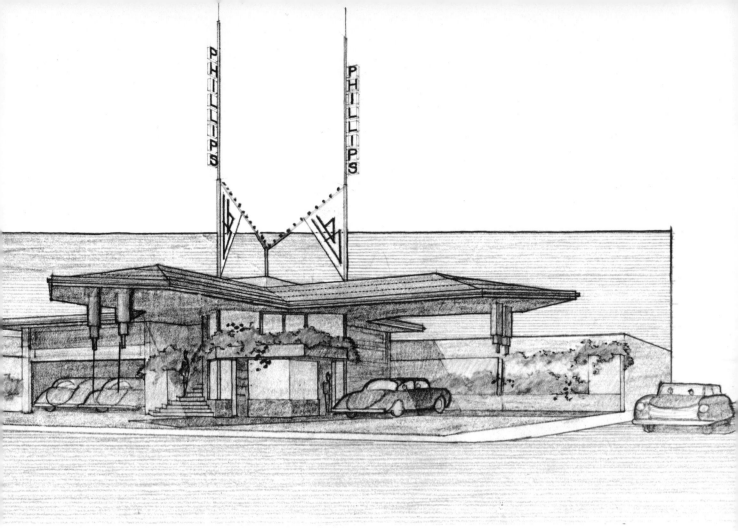

ten to forty minutes of his own home—all now available to him by means of private car or plane, helicopter or some other form of fast public conveyance; factories in which to make his living. Such integrated distribution of living all related to ground—this composes the new city embracing this entire country: the Broadacre City of tomorrow. The city becomes the nation.

When every man, woman, and child may be born to put his feet on his own acres and every unborn child finds his acre waiting for him when he is born—then democracy will have been realized. By way of education made organic, life organic and organic architecture become the greatest servants of modern man. Great architects will surely then develop creative buildings

119

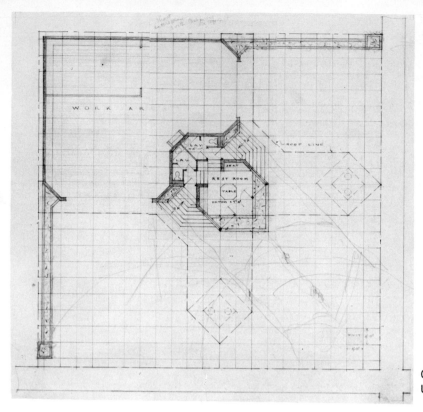

OVERHEAD SERVICE STATION,
UPPER LEVEL PLAN

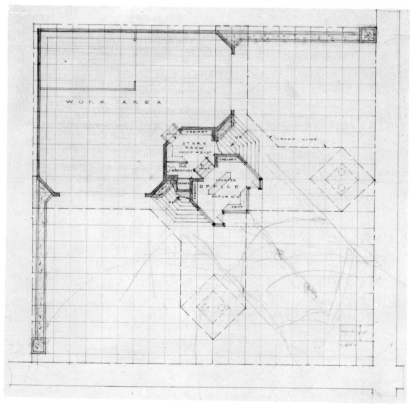

GROUND LEVEL PLAN

not only in harmony with greenery and ground but in intimate patterns of the personal lives of individual owners. No two homes or gardens, none of the farm units of one, two, three—ten acres to forty or more—no two farmsteads be like factory buildings or markets be like either. None need be alike. Nor would any belie its true purpose; nor be ugly. "Styles" no longer fashionable, style itself will have a chance to flourish everywhere. Style now indigenous.

Strong, well built but light and appropriate houses would be good "housing," perhaps prefabricated but spacious workplaces, all of which would be convenient, each sympathetically built out of materials native to the Time, the Place, and the Man. Building construction would be so designed as to take full advantage of Nature. Professor and farmer, factory worker and doctor, entertainer or broker—as well as millionaire—all together in the new city would live and work in environment becoming to each, according to their various needs and nature but none the less themselves superior. All could live close to work or to pleasures. Only a short ride (in time scale) to work in attractive workplaces called factories, to reach markets, travel stations—smokeless; noiseless. Of course the farmer no longer envying the urban dweller or vice verse. His own convenient improvements preferable while the white-collarite in turn might covet the farmer's green pastures and splendid animals although they could now belong to him also should he so make up his mind.

Normally the factory, farm, office, store or dwelling, church or theater would be within ten minute radius of vast, variegated wayside markets and schools. Food fresh every hour and manufactures in markets so placed that each might serve the others effectively, all directly serving appropriate population living or working in easy range of its neighborhood. No need then for the futile racing to and from any far away common center, tired out but racing back and forth again to race again tomorrow. No more stalling off time and crucifixion, just to keep things from being congested and too "big" because of the pacing of some money-making system eventuating from and into the money-trust. Instead of the big fixations of banking and insurance would rise multiplicity of fluid small individual charming human establishments. Freedom at last economic!

Forever fresh air, food no less fresh, sunlight, good land, green underfoot and appropriate spaciousness round about, people building themselves in everywhere, a more moral human life would thrive and develop. So would we live! So, recognizing our possibilities and comparing them with facts as we are all beginning to do (except insurance, the university and capitalism) Usonian home life will not eliminate any of the gadgetry related to modern comfort. It will keep alive and utilize the health-giving machine facilities to which the new freedom is largely due. Steel, glass, plastics too, will be sensibly called upon to fulfill rational uses. Steel for strength and lightness; glass for air-enclosing of interior space, wall screens to make of living in any Usonian house a delightful privacy, give protection against sun, without losing sky and surrounding elements: yes. And the neighbors? Well, their homes should be in no vulgarizing exposure or inconvenient proximity. They would all be in spacious outdoor gardens; their every garden an outdoor home.

Tall buildings? Not barred. No, but they would stand free of neighbors in small green-parks of their own, set in the countryside. Wherever desirable. "Cooperative" apartment houses might be erected for immured, untrained urbanites desiring to enjoy the beauty of the country but yet unable to participate in creating or operating it. But apartment houses need no longer be tier on tier of glass used as curtain walls, but each extended level with its flowers—a vine-festooned balcony-terrace. These semi-public buildings would be conveniently set up in spacious gardens on ground in the outskirts of a neighborhood. All varied activities now similarly independent of crowding would be so placed and built—each presentable to all. Especially schools and hospitals would be but one story high in segregated units.

No man content to build for himself by taking away from others natural rights to space, privacy and light: the result never a monstrosity like today's typical mercantile success, those massive urban apartments.

What life did this immense inhumane toll-gatherer, this nervous, fearsome mantrap which the city raised so high, have to give? What has such success to give any worthwhile citizen, now that he has the motorcar, while in spacious land "out there" the great hard-road systems of our country beckon erstwhile tenants of the cubicle to freedom where his motor may stand not only by his gate but wherever he goes, while he has access to everything he needs in order to live a useful and happy family life on his own ground. The individual truly sovereign!

Everywhere now human voice and vision are annihilating distance—pene-

122

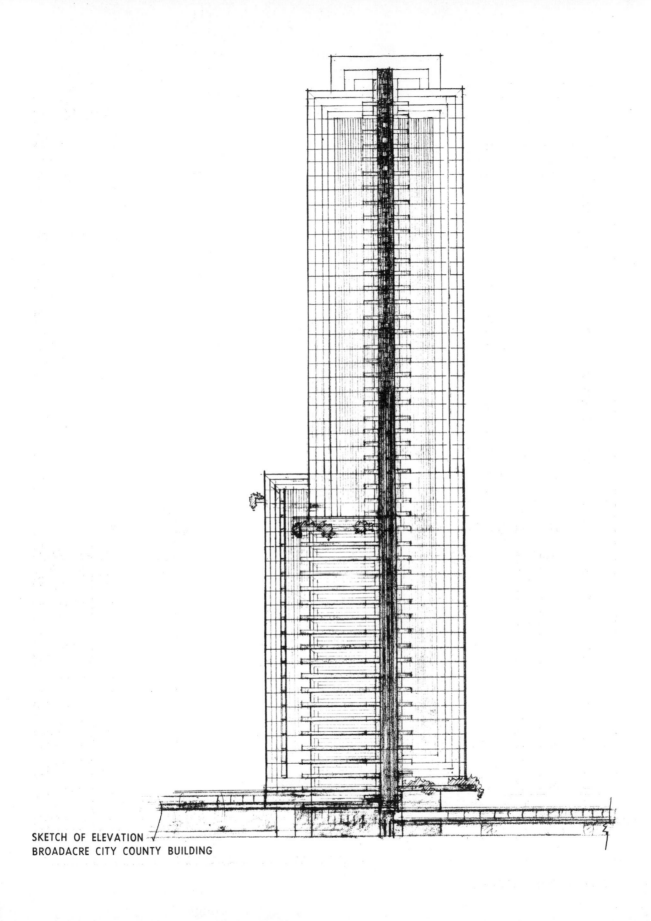

SKETCH OF ELEVATION
BROADACRE CITY COUNTY BUILDING

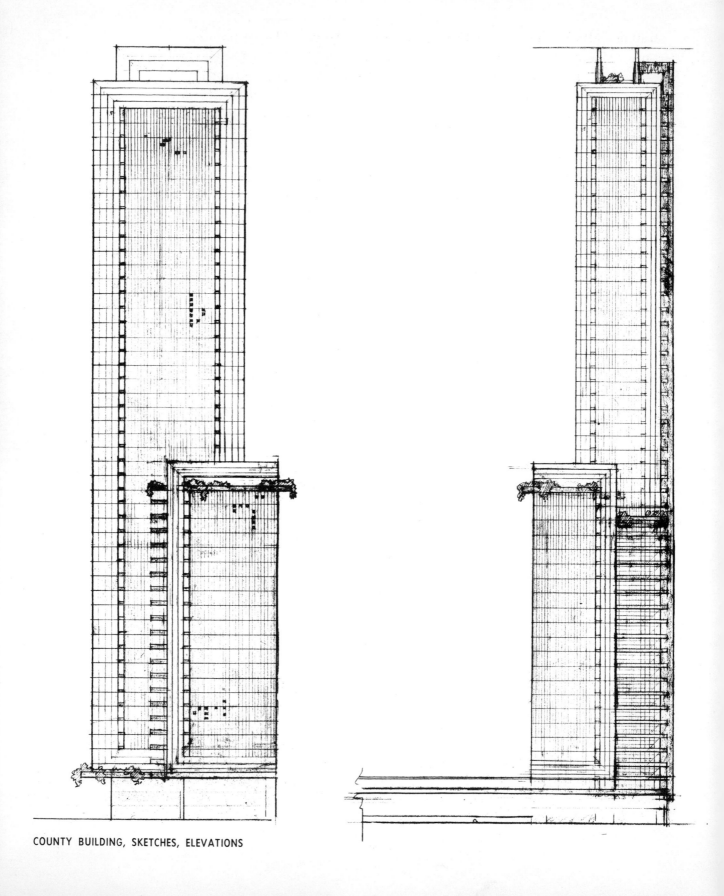

COUNTY BUILDING, SKETCHES, ELEVATIONS

trating walls. Wherever the citizen goes (even as he goes) he has information, lodging and entertainment. He may now be within easy reach of general or immediate distribution of everything he needs to have or to know: All that he may require as he lives becomes not only more worthy of him and his freedom but convenient to him now wherever he may choose to make his home.

I see this Usonian freedom as his "way out there" in a home more than a convenience: I see it as the modern sanctuary. Wherever the citizen wants to be, I see his own beautiful house economically produced by the factory going to the house, not by the house going to the factory—his dwelling in place produced economically and better designed than is his motorcar. By devotion to machinery a few hours a day he should get his house where he wants it. But wherever his home stands it will be a harmonious feature of unviolated environment. And the factory in which he may work, in which he leaves home to go to work, is so built, subdivided and operated throughout in harmonious proportions to his new life, that work is an equally attractive feature not too far away from his own home. An establishment just as becoming to the countryside as is the civic center or church. The time and money that the white-collarite now spends going to and from work, now usefully spent in the diversified colorful activities in the workman's widened margin of leisure in happier circumstances. See these more spacious, comfortable free establishments where whole families play and work; or the modern small farms; all industrial workers not so far from these many small diversified farm-units themselves. But they might own them too; bring their children up in knowledge of nature to help raise produce for highwayside markets which the citizens continually pass; picking up food continually fresh—clients of the professional man who himself comes from far and near to his own clinic built beside his own house. Both now on his own home ground. The modern motorcar will no longer be a stupid, awkward compromise with the horse and buggy to resemble a ferry boat. I see it distinguished as a swift really mobile *machine—humanized.* The only thing mobile about it now? The name.

Arts and crafts of eager, growing, young work-life more conveniently established wherever willed by the citizens—homes, shops, and workshops of craftsmen—artists everyone of them with his own car or air-rotor or both

125

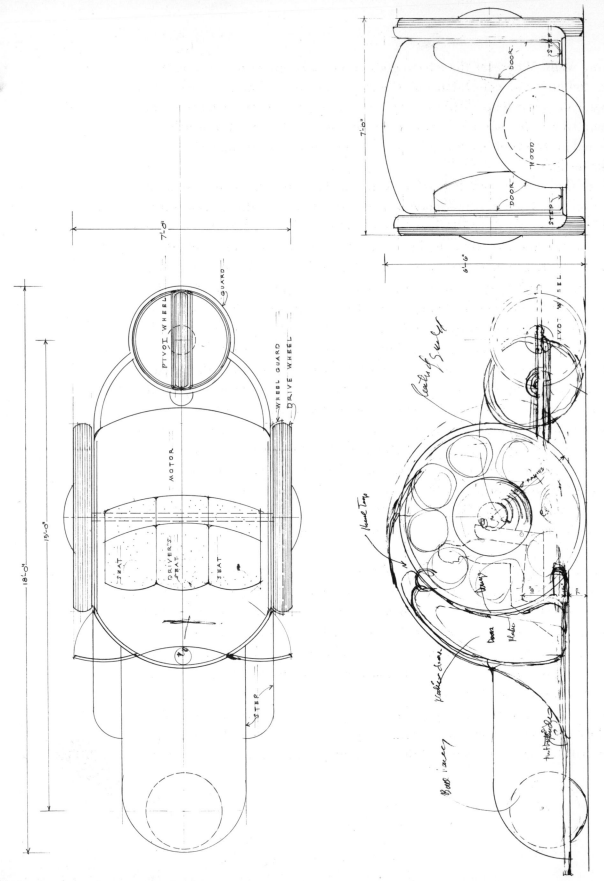

NEW MOTOR CAR DESIGN. VERTICAL BODY BALANCED BETWEEN TWO GREAT WHEELS. STEERING BY TILLER. POWER APPLIED FROM POWER PLANT AT REAR DIRECTLY TO AXLE OF GREAT WHEELS. FUEL AND ENGINE ENSURING GRAVITY. FRONT SPHERICAL WHEEL ENSURING STABILITY AND SHORT TURNS. (IF A TAXI: DRIVER IS ABOVE, A LA HANSOM CAB, AS IN DRAWING BELOW)

TYPICAL STREET VIEW AT CIVIC CENTER WITH NEW TYPE VERTICAL BODY CAR AND HELICOPTER TAXI IN FLIGHT. STREET LIGHTS, SEEN AT INTERVALS LOW ON CURBS, ARE PLACED ALTERNATELY OPPOSITE TO EACH OTHER. IN DISTANCE, UNIVERSAL (NON-SECTARIAN) CATHEDRAL. TOWER AT RIGHT, COMBINATION APARTMENTS AND OFFICES

in addition to fast, regular public transport; these independent in the many small studios and workshops that will abound throughout the city.

I see "going places" a *genuine* luxury; enlightened pleasure in charming places to which all can go at will, so designed; and such places everywhere reserved nearby for occasions. And because the margin of leisure has been doubled by appropriate uses of the machine—and no more back and forth haul—all may have time enough to enjoy them. Droves of happy healthy children go to smaller and ever growing smaller schools. Garden-schools are more numerous and more individual. I see children there in their own little practice-shops working in little individual vegetable and flower gardens, schools and hospitals set in parks that are near garden playgrounds, placed where nature periodically stages "a beautiful show." Raising vegetables and animals of all kinds. Many joys now yet to be known would be a commonplace experience.

I see children's parents meantime living the free individual life that would enrich the communal life by the very changing quality of their own fresh individuality. And last of all but not least, I see beauty in the new life unafraid of anything outside itself: life that has rediscovered faith in life by

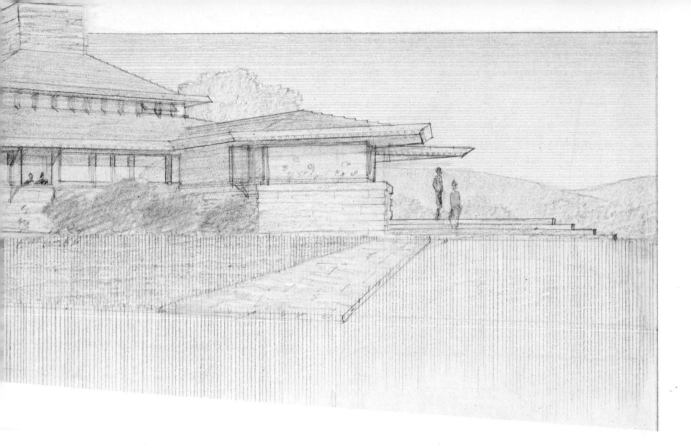

faith in itself. All this harmony with nature in varied transport, buildings, work and recreation spaciously intimate with liberated transport I see as the proper life of the proper city. A great Usonian agronomy instead of the heartless sterilizing cinder-strip of enormous "industrialization," production senselessly increasing production only for the sake of more production.

Plan and elevation would all be carefully thought out in all establishments, as appropriate to purpose as each is to the other. Liberal life made free to flow from each to each. So to every man his life according to his natural ability, his choice free, the life of all suited to normal need. We might have had all this long ago.

With each generation this fresh outward flow from the lives of liberated citizens naturally refreshed and duly increased. Everywhere in America this warm upsurging of life is our heritage: a nation truly free to use its own great woods, hills, fields, meadows, streams, mountains and wind-blown sweeps of the vast plains all brought into the service of men and women in the name of mankind: Doing all this, doing no violence to get it done, America justly proud of its own organic power and beauty. Citizens under-

129

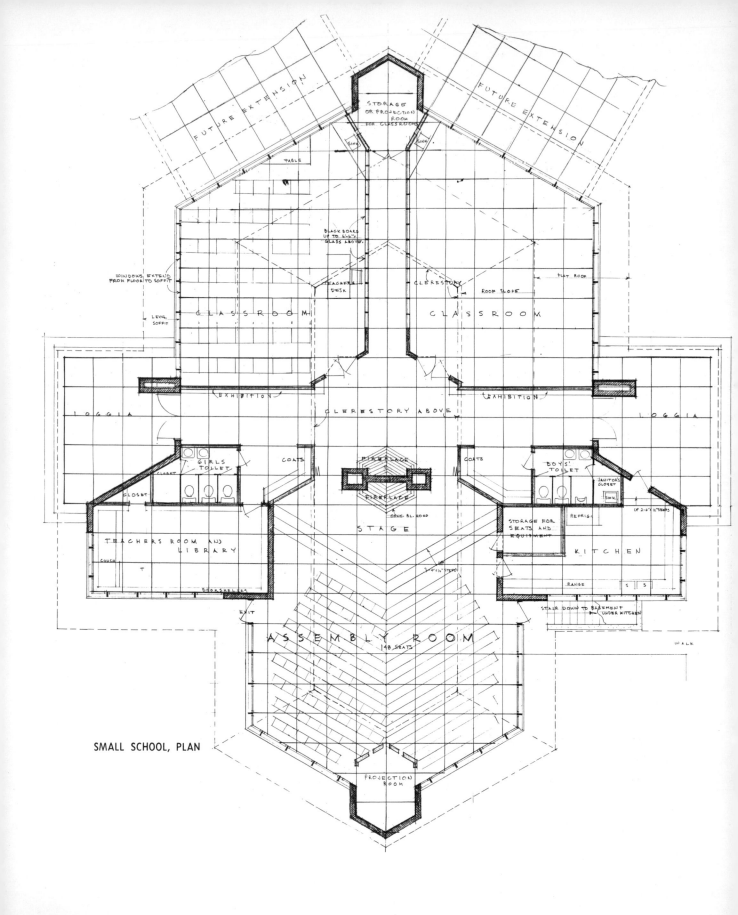

SMALL SCHOOL, PLAN

standing and conserving all natural resources whether of material or men. This—to me—is the proper service to be rendered by the architects of our country—the service of organic architecture to the democratic life of Usonia! Architecture alive: the cultivator of youth—preserver of the beauty of nature —guide and counselor of the growing American family as well as conservator of crops, flocks and herds. The philosophy of organic architecture looks— and sees these all together as the field in which the architect is born to practice.

From coast to coast and border to border, the hangover of ancient ambitious centralization has now left the vast new acreage of these United States a neglected backyard. Smoke-and-cinder-gas-blighted areas make drear ground the industrial revolution has left in its wake; especially in the East and lake region. The South wears permanent scars. Permanent scars on both Man and Nature are the eternal shame of the industrialism that rose to power in the North from the cinder heaps. So many billions have already been wasted upon our becoming the arsenal of a fortuitous life. We are vainly trying to keep up at such great cost the "price system" that ran away; we called it "industrial revolution!" A pity that all this increment could not have been spent to create a more fruitful example of a truly liberal democratic life. What irony! Peace has never been organized for the innate glory of America—only for or against war! Or the fear of war.

Dying, Napoleon said, "Why has force never been able to organize anything?" Already, how often proved?

And, yet, just because forces of peace have never been truly organized (how magnificent they might be!) the freedom guaranteed by the Constitution of the U. S. A. has not only never been achieved but seldom understood. Were peace really organized as war is now organized, war could never defeat peace on any terms whatsoever. Citizens of Broadacre City will not be afraid that "peace will break out."

War would look as sinister to children and the citizen called upon to wage it as it really is. The teenager and the citizen would soon compel "the interests" to pay the price for peace in terms of peace and by their own contribution.

Human imagination is capable of greater divinity than we now realize.

It alone is able to distinguish the human herd by way of the character that is individuality, able eventually to save man from the fate that has overtaken, finally, all previous human herds by way of their own civilization.

Finally, I see this release and increase of our native resources all adding up to a grand free culture of a civilization made integral with Nature by a noble architecture of its own: architecture by and for manhood, making the machine the proper means to create nobler longings in man for more fruitful activities than our new world has yet seen.

Let us then free ourselves from all secret government of our lives, from official artificiality; and let us free ourselves from false theories as to how we would or should act subsequently. But, what will the nation that is an organic comprehensive new city be like if we would thus design and build it instead of letting it, as now, haphazard, build itself? Abundance exists in Nature's own kind and time. Fruitfulness is abounding; not diminishing but increasing.

So the regenerate Broadacres architect enters now as master of utilization: as house-planner, road-builder, bridge-builder, town-planner and planter. The superhighway, tributary hard roads and bridges being—more than ever —fundamental architectural factors. Everywhere new dispensations are compelling, by discipline from within, a quickening sense of all this in the new city capital of the natural order of organic Democracy.

Low sweeping grades, banked turns on surfaced roadbeds, no open ditches beside the roads, wherever possible hedges for fences, well-considered green-covered cuts and fills healed by good planting of indigenous ground cover. All may have supreme beauty. Moving road-lines that are the highways laid down sympathetic to terrain, threading hills and plains with safe grades everywhere; these are already a delightful circumstance. Wherever they occur they are elemental features of architecture. Sightly road protections will be well studied together with designed drainage; culverts and bridges, in themselves, designed as good architecture. Where concrete retaining walls would be prohibitive in cost there could be lines of blocks dotted along the sloping banks of every turn. Evergreen masses by the mile would line the roads for snow protection, instead of unsightly snow fences. Masses of native growth would sweep over banks of the cut or fill,

132

not the usual collection of so many different kinds of shrubs and trees misnamed landscape architecture. Everywhere possible, without obstructing desirable views, would be broad sweeps of native trees. At many an appropriate place always an eye to bloom and color changing with the seasons. Safe roads for hilly or flat country; curved roads always for curved country and contour tillage of all sloping fields. Everywhere, no trucks on main roads nor wires on poles. "Public service" safely underground.

No main hard road in the new city would have less than four lanes, some of them double-decked. Superhighways should have no less than six lanes with over- and under-passes for traffic. Nor should any ditches for drainage be allowed open alongside. "Roads be concave, not convex," become low-lighted ribbons at night, service pipes laid down at the center in concrete open trenches. Fueling-and-servicing-stations would be found at wayside parks and at strategic highway intersections. Road construction and green-planting, both as engineering and architecture, would be (naturally enough) under control of each county seat in every state, but with the best supervision that supervising architects, landscape architects and structural engineers afford. The very best that this country, or perhaps the world, affords would not be too good, and would become *official*. Each main county seat would receive special attention. At proper points along or under railways or highways safe, spacious underground refuge should be constructed for the various kinds of storage uses in peacetime. These might afford protection under attack from the air; making such attack unprofitable.

The modern architect's trained sense of the harmonious "altogether" in these several matters of road construction, planting, bridge-building, would, and from beginning to end, be indispensable to the integrity of the conception of the whole universal city. A perfected agronomy in the best sense everywhere on the way.

Romans built such great roads that to this day they remain. But with the systems of reinforced concrete we now practice and our modern machines, we could as cheaply build better, more lasting roads and make all factors in a noble architectural scheme. What nobler agent has culture or civilization than the great open road made beautiful and safe for continually flowing traffic, a harmonious part of a great whole life?

Along these grand roads as through human veins and arteries throngs city life, always building, building, planning, working; living nearby or coming from miles away in these independent, cooperative broad-acres that are growing to be a greater nation than any ever lived in before.

Native lakes and streams, mountain resorts, all made more easily available by private plane or air motorization. Transport could thus contribute no small element of pleasure to our life. The barge and small motorboats could do in relation to the land for rivers and large bodies of water what the plane has done for the land itself.

The bad form of centralism that built the great railway stations as gateways to the old city (*Bahnhof*) will be gone. Exaggeration of conspicuous waste in any form will bear manifest rebuke by society. There may be many minor transient stations instead of a few major ones because "the great station," owing to lack of the great concentration, is no longer desirable. As flight develops, air-rotor or helicopter depots will be connected with the cross country rights-of-way on which once were laid the hard rails, trucks now running each side these rails. Railway cars would not run by noisy "trucks" but slide down shallow skids, the cars mounted upon them being light cylindrical tubes—perhaps jet-powered. A railway train would become capable of 150 miles an hour without any uncomfortable vibration. New traffic systems would include contact systems with minor flight-stations, and be placed wherever a flight-station might be regarded as permissible or convenient. The big terminal and storage warehouses of the present would not exist as eyesores because all would disappear beneath the tracks except at ports of entry or export; the major part of the traffic business, of either gathering or distribution of freight now free to go from rails to house or hand to hand. From factory and farm to family or from family to factory—piecework becomes no mere slogan but a reality. Or from producer to exporter, or from importer to distributing center, by way of the universal traffic lanes to which all units of either production or consumption have quick and easy access. Wasteful back-and-forth haul eliminated by good planning. As the natural city grows in completeness distribution is more and more easy.

But there will always be particular concentrations at ports and mines. A port concentration will differ from that of the inland city. Every such concentration will have imposed upon it the particular character of its special environment and situation, therefore each will differ from the others. One-third of all railroad business at present is hauling coal but now coal will be transformed into electricity at the mines: power lines and pipelines all underground. Water power is everywhere utilized to complete general electrifications all now available as a public asset, service at cost to the people. Atomic power the possession of the people when it comes.

Such individual differences as lie within the general shape and purposes of the universal city would all be naturally developed as *architecture* except wherever conformity to uniformity of mass production might enter as substantial human benefit. Standardization—and its usual bureaucracy—might be the warp of a nation woven as would be a variegated, appropriate fabric. The ultimate weaving in all standardizing need show no less imagination and individuality than ever if in the hand of the creative architect. But because of the Machine used as a tool the finished whole might have the richer variety of individuality and so have finer quality than yet imagined. This inevitable individual differentiation of character as form and form as idea would give fascination to all of life: everywhere charm!

See that very human quality of individuality—strange to say, a quality these United States of America are finding it difficult to recognize, utilize and preserve: a quality we have all but lost, yet evident as the precious core of all creative power. Owing to no vicarious living whatever, nor to any false vainglorious success-ideal depending too much upon a too vicarious means by way of which man now surrenders in order to survive. Mere employment in the new city is by no means enough! Human satisfactions must be freed from the tyranny of stock plan-and-rule government; we must learn to recognize lapses of democracy even before we have learned to know what democracy really is. To conquer lawlessness in some other country, why must we submit to bureaucratic impositions here at home? What future for us then except as servile to brutal power as much as we are its beneficiaries?

When atomic power gets out of uniform—into overalls—fuel, public or private, for all purposes will be turned into electricity at the mines wherever sources of power are needed; or oil or gas pipelined to places. Power from all sources relayed underground to the consumer. Electrification thus universal will be low in cost. Atomic power really owned by the citizen will not only be able to compete but will abolish everything else as the source of heat, light and power.

Great power-transmission units underground and pipe lines where necessary would be the same miracles of modern engineering as the shoes we wear. Wherever natural resources happened to abound there improved methods of making power available to the citizen would take all fuel or power underground.

Awakened sense of the value of our native landscape would use so many recent developments in wireless telegraphy and telephone now unfairly suppressed, and make all poles and wires overhead a bad memory of ugliness and danger. This ruthless scaffolding once upon a time disfiguring environment by way of public service companies, hanging and maiming the countryside for all citizens for most of a century—these will not be found in the new city. This imposition of crude, utilitarian scaffolding, incurred during the infancy of our haphazard growth as a mechanized nation, invariably does violence to our own character as well as the countryside, violates to this day all the finer sensibilities of American life. Such crudity disappears in Usonia. Power and traffic will have found avenues of distribution more conservative of the general interest and found economical popular distribution in wiser, more public-spirited methods. Such devices as are now termed "service"—swept from sight into general discard, together with poles, wires, hard rails, track elevations, dirt overpasses, gas plants, coal-burning powerhouses, train sheds, roundhouses, coal yards, lumber and building material yards—all go out or under. These ugly features of life today no longer needed except under cover of road elevation in the groundwork of traffic systems themselves. Unsightly structures could nowhere exist in this new city of the future. Evidences of these crude if fundamental ways of money-making our pioneering days accepted are seen no more. Obtrusive, offensive scaffolding of any kind will be taken down so that the culture of our civilization may now appear, though as late as the middle of the twentieth century.

Such are the general *topographical* elimination and distributing features of the free city that decentralization itself is building among us right now, without our help or any wise planning, or anything at all but hindrance from the official finance-powers we are operating. *Organic reintegration* must follow decentralization. Planning is the factor that will develop the new city and keep the city economical and beautiful. The new Broadacres will absorb all needless cities and towns where they stand. The many big ones so badly overbuilt by the ruthless clinging to capitalistic centralizations making crowding profitable because crowding is made indispensable. The flowering of the new city, as we may see, depends upon the great topographical road systems for ubiquitous mobility. We can see them everywhere growing around us; well underway is the universal traffic problem. In Broadacres such jamming of various parts? Non-existent.

So these changing interpretations of American democracy through culture at last on good terms with education, will make the modern City not only a free city but a finer, a beautiful city—a city serving American ideals of freedom which might with all justice be called democracy building democracy.

Now, how do the various buildings themselves, human units in the new liberal planning by and for the reflex, become valid expressions of modern life? If with true aesthetic sensibility we should scientifically see in perspective the vast resources with which we continually go to war but with which we have certainly never learned how to go into creative work: Invention? Yes. Creation—no. Were we to see our own wasted forces organized for peace, we would find that the greatest benefits to come from the free city might come from men not "employed" in the old sense at all but men who work freely because they like doing what they do. "Employment," being free, now grows and does more than "stay in line" in some vast money-making game, on a wage-scale all out of proportion with the new time-scale brought to the surface by the leverage of Science.

Once consumption as master really faces production down, work takes on different character: Quality then has a chance to become accepted as superior to quantity, and it would naturally be so.

As a matter of course, the new standard of spacing by time-scale vitally affects everything in our new general city plan. These effects appear in every building—in every major or minor detail of this conscious elimination of the tyrannical major and minor axes in order to be free to plan according to Nature. Here we have at last the elimination of the insignificant.

Thus we shall see entirely new forms for living; and see a finer, more secure family life. We will see integrity of means to ends, the individual we have been prophesying and promoting we shall see taking effect in more intelligently civilized constructions. Men would build from the heart as well as by the head: build either by hand or by machine, but build always from the good ground upward and from the inside outward to comprehend time, place and man.

Most important, then, to us as a people would be this fast-clearing fact that the means to live a more lovable life now demands a more livable city. This Broadacre concept of city-planning simply means that any building in any place, of whatever kind, is concerned first with the new sense of space in spaciousness and of the nature appropriate to purpose and materials and tools. The old standards of spacing should have gone out when universal mobility and electrification came in. This concept of "planning" is a matter of the right kind of building in the right way in the right place for the right people. The individual has already secured speed and comparative flight. No mere expensive stunt. By more experimentation with mechanical powers, modern man may secure even more vicarious power. But it is now clear that he has acquired certain propensities of the bird as he had already acquired certain propensities of animals and fish. Security for him in this changed cycle of time now lies in use of the vicarious powers more naturally characteristic of his better self in a free city. A vast new city perceived according to deeper elementals enlarging his life with perception of his spirit according to his new advantages—using all machine powers, land, and sound money as mere tools by means of which he builds an architecture for life not as now lived, not by vain exaggerations and murderous neglects and abuses to destroy and be himself destroyed, but to build a great City. To be of the twentieth century this city must be built in these comprehensive terms of organic spiritual need instead of the *meum et tuum* of a profit system. As financial gain is now set it may be considered a public need. Money should have no power whatever in itself, as no commodity at all with which to merely speculate should have a credit value. It should have value only as a *medium* of exchange.

To develop organic power, to overcome these brittle economic obstructions continually thrown in the way of development by the present terms of orthodox finance, creative architecture must make available for its Place, Time and Man the various forms within which we may truly better live and build and make a great life now possible to us. If life is to be lived consistent with our great new powers and the widening margin of leisure (both now in infancy), both to be a blessing not a curse, man must be able immeasurably to widen his own spiritual horizon and exercise his spiritual capacity accordingly.

Again, consider the fact that machine increment by movement is far different from man moving on his legs or driving a horse-drawn vehicle. This new standard of measurement must be applied to any general plan-spacing in space-planning of the new city and its new homes. More important, this new space concept enters to be directly applied not only to buildings themselves but with equal constructive force to the mind and conscience of man himself. The sense of lived-in space within the building must be clearly seen as reality: Space-building being the kind of building available to him now. The sense of space *within* as the reality of building is not a new concept; it is ancient essential principle not only necessarily implied by the ideal of democracy itself but inherent first in the philosophy of Laotze and then in the nature-studies of Jesus.

Time is now for us to interpret this eternal sterling principle with our command of modern mechanical equipment, so to make the life of any building *actual* instead of allowing it to grow more and more a vicarious tax on reality. This should be established as profound *architectural* philosophy.

Now, along with steel and the use of a great variety of thin sheets of metal and wood comes greater demand for economical and appropriate use of materials not only new but old as well. This is for light, widely spanned spaces, exposures closed against the elements but not closed except at will to light and air, prospect-vista retained where desired.

Here, then, enters the new significances for the new City with liberating super-materials like glass and steel.

See the architecture of heavy enclosure for human life (the fortification) vanishing! A new kind of building to take its place comes to view—like magic—building now more natural to our time. In spite of all untoward vicarious circumstance, man is now to be less separated from nature. The new citizen is to be, in every way, a deeper man in the life of his own time. The hard and fast lines between outside and inside (where he is concerned) tend to disappear. Any building—outside—may come inside and the inside go outside when each is seen as part of the other and a part of the landscape. Continuity, plasticity, and all these imply, are fast coming home to him—a miraculous new release in life as well as architecture. The reflex democratic is now to be his in place of the captious strictures of monarchic power or the major and minor axes in which he was imprisoned by the "classic" bondage of centuries à la Renaissance as interpreted by the Paris Beaux Arts.

This interior difference is all the difference.

The king is dead; long live the king! But now the king is his majesty—the American citizen.

A new superlative is the basis of our new city for the new world not alone in architecture but no less so in the world of thought. Not only is *building* now free to be natural in and to America but so are the new space realizations of the new city themselves free. Modern man therefore no less free. Liberality now lies in properly awakened consciousness of our new circumstances. To be free will become *natural*: no longer freedoms ("the five freedoms") counted out to the man on the fingers of one hand. Freedom is of all, for all.

The fixations of traditional forms never knew such exhilarating release. If ancient forms are imitated, they can only interfere and destroy. All the traditional forms we ever knew were but external mass-concepts—facades for an external life under some form of conscription. Exterior compulsion. Exterior pressures exerted upon men to whom congestion was no unmixed evil. An "exterior" architecture. Actually congestion was not only a great convenience but necessary to the impositions of authority.

Mis-education

Congestion has grown monstrous. The new principle and the natural changes we face are the important facts—the true basis of the art of beautifully building organic buildings is now a great *machine-age economy!* Economy *organic* in itself beautiful. Economy is at last an element of beauty where each is of each other; they should be as *one.* Our civilization may at last rise to its best and bravest by way of such wisdom and democratic man demand to be ruled by what is seen by him only as bravest and best in his life.

Drastic congestions of mass centralization devastate the free growth of individual man's spiritual life. All old traditional forms must no longer be allowed to interfere with our new life. As a nation we are suffering from a low glut of population and *things;* things without beauty; people without spirit. This is reflected in our buildings. We have suffered untold hindrance to culture by way of popular "taste"; we suffer now from lifters of the little finger, who promulgate their own taste as arbiters of art and architecture. "Taste" becomes the false criterion, now that we may learn of architecture as organic. It was "taste" that made our culture a parasite, or parody, and helped our present city to be what it is today? Degenerate?

Some of our better factory buildings, escaping the facade, are already exempt from the academic excess made by commercial success. We are suffering yet from the so-called monumental and official building: academic hangovers that we said were in the "classic" tradition, merely reproductions of feudal thinking. This "classic" so narrowly fixed as "style" by current mis-education upon young minds. As the acquisitive jackdaw plunders to line his nest, or as our monkey-psychology still glorifies "to have and to hold," so cults in our great nation are especially servile. It is fabulous waste of the young when they are not allowed to be elevated to the study of all categories of Nature organic in art.

And, too, the fashionable house of the past period-of-the-periods was not only a sodden box-mass of some kind—masses of building material punched full of holes "à la" some dessicated mode or ancient fashion recorded by the museums—but often the result of mania for the antique which made of every house a bazaar, a museum, or junk shop. This disgrace to culture was set up here at home as authority by men who, in this remote darkness of the now obsolete shadow-of-the-wall, were themselves mere "left-overs."

Let us declare that this new era of freedom for which we hope and here prophesy is dawning in our hitherto servile American architecture—at last —although "possession" of the profit-system still operates as a scab on a festering sore. Democratic privilege, our heritage from the past, sinks to lowest terms in our politics. As for culture, what good sense there was in "the Colonial" style still survives as simian mimicry in the eclecticisms of many of our domestic establishments. Everywhere this "style complex" originally came from buildings that were no more than personal realizations, and foolish confessions (or else professions), of an inferiority complex mistaking itself for refinement or "the fashion."

This servility in architecture was proof enough that architects themselves as merchants of these backyard "styles" were all the architects the average American householder knew or had a chance to patronize—until organic architecture appeared. But any citizen capable of consecutive thought may now (and therefore) take hold of modern life problems with a share in them himself. Yes, one's own life problem (it is usually and chiefly a building) is able to obtain light from within. Independent study and real appreciation of organic law may now reach him if he will. The Usonian citizen may soon think his own way through to the particular share in the solution of this problem that is really his own. We are impelled to build this new city if we desire salvation for our civilization. The City of Broadacres is dedicated to him.

To Begin

Beginning at the beginning is apparently an art in itself long lost. This ideal Usonian citizen will now find all proper proportions and significance in this word "organic." It is only a biological term which might indicate something hanging in the butcher shop; but it also indicates where part is to part as part is to whole. But before it is truly significant we must realize *form and function as one*. A spiritual truth instead of a mere fact.

This sense of the organic in the realm of the spirit is a secret of simplicity itself. Organic architecture in this sense is able to create a form of life that will pull many a puzzled mind out of dull academic confusion, open many new doors to this greatest of all arts—architecture—to the human spirit. The mind thus opened will enable democratic freedom of the individual to become a realization.

Erstwhile fashionable period architects and their fashionable clients have now tried every phase of abnegation to styles of the past. Shoddy pretenses. During their better moments such architects have tried to imbue their clients with a simplicity merely pictorial. Now they may try for simplicity genuine. Or, let's say, simplicity natural. There can never be anything organic about imitation whatsoever, either going or coming.

Change Will Take Effect

In every phase of the present order there is static; it is fixation that seems to be needed, but release is coming: coming from the source of power nearest to us "ourselves." If abused, abused by our own consent. This potential source of power plus the machine will become chief means to our desired liberation. But should we fall to imitating machines in planning our buildings, even if inspired by steamships, automobiles, airplanes, bathtubs, refrigerators, and water closets, then comes the streamline dogma—novel but dogma all over again. This time the dogma is the cliché "Form follows Function."

Now negation is not necessarily fatal. Neither is waste necessarily so. But negation sterilizes after all, and is only another phase of simplicity merely pictorial. If we dig deeper into Nature we will soon understand that simplicity is as far as the lilies of the field beyond any affected pictorialism. But as a beginning negation has already helped clean up the rubbish heap encumbering our architecture. Negation may be no more than a passing service.

Nevertheless the urban citizen's one-piece bathtub and water-closet do come nearer to beauty than do his present facades by pictorialism. And the car standing at the door shames the house if for no other reason than that in design it is itself a sham.

The intelligence that renounces the period house will also reject the foolish exaggeration in the design of the present car. But try to find a house with the integrity of the new reality. A house or a car integral with Time, Place, and Man.

Beginning to build the free city democracy demands that the young architect search for intimacy with actual building on the good ground. It will result in fruitful service on his part to the fundamentals by his very devotion to himself in his art. Realization of principle in practice will grow creative competence in place of the prevalent scholastic impotence. The soul of America is not yet dead in the young. The young architect will learn to build again as great folk-masters once built, as the songmasters of music wrote—out of the man himself for love of his art.

As things go with us, and with the young architect especially, negation is often good medicine—is so in all the arts—and may do something to abolish the culture faker by awakening and broadening a general dislike for him and a desire for simplicity, although the negator himself may be a culture faker. Even within our cerebral academic system—wherein youth is now educated so far beyond his capacity as to be highbrow—we may see change.

And whenever we do reach the true interior order of simplicity we will still find, among other motley dubious assets, offices inherited from the passing "order of the schools." Find the enormous armies of front-runners, "go-getters," peddlers, brokers, designing-partners, inferior desecrators and feature-writers, journalists, advertising agencies and professors: merchants all. All doing some kind of brokerage between the client (or purchaser) and his own abilities. Again and afresh, it is these quondam "experts" who become parasites in and upon the present aged city. Vain hope that the bureaucracy and academic tutelage that have made such weaklings socially acceptable will ever put fair premiums upon the integrity of the organic qualities in man. If we confound personality with individuality, we will never be able to put the right premiums in the right place; upon individuality whether in philosophy, religion, science, architecture or art.

But America needs no help to Broadacre City. It will haphazard build itself. Why not plan it?

We will be unable to save our immediate phase of civilization from present distortion or eventual destruction by the ambitious merchant-scientist,

144

merchant-architect or the merchants of the "industrial revolution" or the merchants of the far more important chemical revolution. Why all these merchants!

The creative artist? Well—naturally he is himself one who by nature is as important to society as society is important to itself. Which should mean that he is by nature (and by office) the qualified leader in any society, natural, native interpreter of the visible forms of any socal order in or under which we choose to live. If worthy to be so accepted, happily so. If rejected by our society, it will be because society will not learn to see the true radical as the romanticist he is. The romanticist we are bound to discover as the true realist; to see the creative artist, then, as modern seer of the poetic principle. Not only is he way-shower but, with experienced command of modern ways and means, he is our natural leader toward a coveted culture of our own.

Why then, even in our best society, here in these United States, are we so afraid of the radical? Why so afraid of every genuinely creative individuality? Is society so afraid because the spiritual values necessary to see the radical as he is, are undeveloped? And all social economic values go tipsy and twisting down the line? Society is actually afraid of truth? Of course it is, as Society now exists. "Society" is more or less afraid because, whoever the "elite" now are, their cherished prejudices are likely to be their holiest feelings, turned topsy-turvy by the truth sought by the radical. So society depends upon the imposing strong-arm enforcements of authority. The elite must now lose guardianship unless the true concept of the term "organic" dawns for them.

The Word "Organic"

Be warned this word "organic" is like the word "nature." If taken in a sense too biological, it would not be what it is: light in darkness; it would be a stumbling block. The use of the term "organic" in architecture applies to a concept of intrinsic living and of building intrinsic and natural; both concepts seen together in structure as Native. To the young architect the term should be a daily working concept of the great *altogether* wherein features and parts, congenial in form and substance, are applied to purpose as congenital.

Such then is the true significance of the word "organic." We often refer to this quality as "entity."

The Usonian on His Own Acreage

It is not true that the poor are poor because the rich are rich. To say so is an attempt to divert attention from the real causes of poverty. The rich are as parasitic as the poor and probably less able to be happy.

Let us first consider the "poor."

"The poor"? The term immediately raises the "housing problem," now receiving so much social and official attention. Beneficial though some of the attention is, "housing" by our government can only practice putting off, by mitigation of a daily horror, the day of actual regeneration for the poor. Or build poverty into the nation as an institution.

The poor? They are those citizens most hardened, hindered or damaged by inexorable, multiple *rents*. Unearned increment progresses and piles up into the insurance of American fortunes. The poor are poor because of *triple rent:* rent for land, rent for money, rent for ideas. Or else the poor are only the lame, the halt, and the blind, not so numerous.

Where is the place for the poor in these cities and towns built and maintained by makers and takers of triple rent?

For answer, see the salvage effected by the latest and best slum clearance or "housing" developments all over the country, those formidable red brick towers. They are only improved, instead of improvised, slums. No doubt the poverty of the slum-quarter has been built in as an authorized state of body and mind; base standardization of the unproductive human soul. Poverty of spirit thus *builds* poverty into a great liability of our nation! This grim boxing of families—tier on tier—row on row—behind rows or beside rows of other families similarly boxed. Cubicles, the same or similar on rows of shelves on shelves, relentless in military array! Here is no monarchic hang-over but an oppression wholly remote from the reflex of democratic nature

146

and hateful to the student of organic architecture; about as inspiring as any coffin. But now decent? Maybe. But just for that, as things go—a deadening straitjacket in which human life may be "beneficiary"? But not yet blessed. Here we see ingenious regimentation, by government order, of this army of the poor: the poor who are to be poor and *stay* poor "*decently*"? Made poorer by the machine? Yes and no. But made poorer by big-time production's flagrant greed. Here we see the abuse of surplus machine power and orthodox finance going hand in hand to make people useless at a rate soon triumphant: people machine-made in a machine-made world.

Even though "one's own way" (the old slum) may sink to license and stink, is there not more dignity, at least, in the "freedom" with which it sank? But what human dignity is there in the smell of soap and sanitation in these heavy red-brick prison-cells; in all this dull reiteration of no-idea, no feeling here—housings for nobodies, not homes for somebody—this dreary insistence upon *spiritual* poverty as an institution? Even though a bathtub be incorporated and a posy stuck in some flowerbox to decorate this lucrative form of rent—a sinister light is cast by our great industrial and social "success" in this "housing" of the poor, imprisoned for life by way of high-class "insurance."

Why not have especially subsidized transportation? Why not make the land they were surely born by nature to inherit, more free to the growing families of the "poor"? The land they were born to inherit as they were born to inherit air to breathe, daylight to see by, water to drink. Perhaps food to eat? Why not? I am well aware of the academic economist's reaction to any question of free land or anything "free" at all. Anywhere. And on present systems there is plenty of exercise for such rationalisms as his. But Henry George showed us—his people—clearly enough the simple basis of human poverty: the only *organic* solution of the land problem needed by the poor rich or the rich poor. Neither are secure? Any solution of their problem is eventually our own imperative salvation—soon, or we will have no true democratic society. What hope exists for proper stimulation of the great architecture of a great life while owners of land hold all man-made improvements on the land *against* the man on his land, instead of man-made improvements holding the land? For any organic economic structure as a basis for architecture this is wrong end to. Error at the root: that is to say, radically wrong. In present circumstances architecture is only for the landlord—building by permission of the banker.

Some form of redemption (or exemption) and subsequent co-operative sharing of increase in land values is past due to society. Authority must make available to each poor man acreage according to his ability (and the ability of his family) *to make good use of the land*! If at first there must be subsidy, then—again—why not subsidize transportation? And then—what house for the poor man? Where and what assistance may he find to go to work himself to build a home with and for his growing family? Certainly the present city is no place for him—or his—a mantrap for the poor.

Modern mobility can be so easily arranged for these citizens. Rescue and restitution are now ready for "the poor man" in a new city. Especially by way of a bus or a motor car. Emancipated from triple rent and with good ground now made available to him, he—machine-worker now rented, paying toll to the exaggerated city in order that the city give him work to do—should not he, the "poor," a wage-slave, go not backward but forward to his native birthright: the good ground? His family may grow up even well off in this free city? The poor are there to release their initiative; both work-place and family home may be the same and pleasant. Worthy and inspiring, this association. Families, as such, productive on their own ground, with modern scale of time-spacing, they can truthfully say "ten miles is nearby." Even more miles, say twenty. Or more soon.

The poor man? Yes. . . . Usually he is now wage-slave at some machine. He is probably on the production line. Somewhere. Somehow. And because he is there bound to his employers' machine, common sense would say that to use the machine to start building his own home himself he ought to be able soon, even as things are, to buy a standardized privy, cheap. That "privy" civilized is now a bathroom, manufactured complete and delivered to him as a single unit (his car or his refrigerator the same as the privy) all ready to use when connected to the city water system and a fifteen-dollar septic tank or a forty-dollar cesspool. Well advised, he will plant this first unit wherever it belongs to start his home. The other necessary units similarly cheap; bedrooms designed for beneficial living added. As months go by, the rent he saved may buy other standardized units; a comfortable living-room and as many more bedrooms as he needs. These and other well designed prerequisites may be added as soon as he earns them by his work or the work of his family, in nearby agriculture, crafts or mechanized industries. His family, meantime, are helping to maintain themselves free on their own ground. All such standard units, varied in general scheme of assembly to suit either flat land or hillside, in various materials so designed as to make not only a dignified but well-planned appropriate whole. This I know. Such various standardized units as we already have are forbidding merely because they were not designed to take the curse off bad design in repetition, and do not add up to a practical gracious whole. But all are produced ad libitum, ad nauseam, by the machine owners' mastery of labor under a bad standardized "production-controlling-consumption" system working in some prefab-profiteering factory. Standards badly designed because bad design is cheap and good costs money? So the shop hates to pay for intangibles and good design is one of these. But the benefits of the "cheapening" process now seldom go to the worker. They go to the big producer to increase production; and quantity soon wipes out quality. But properly standardized units may be produced in the free city as part of itself! And, like automobiles, be produced by the cheapening power of modern mass production come right-side-up: and operated *on the worker's side*. The small cart no longer before the big horse.

Well then—as our artisan grows in resources, so his home grows. The artisan-home-maker now buys the required parts in some well-planned group-scheme of production that benefits by design from long study by the world's best talent, so minded. And such a flexible group of talent may "standardize" units not only to be harmonized by production to do no outrage to the landscape but also at last to be roomy and cheap enough to the consumer—so that his rent for three months in city bondage would buy the first units of his home if the machine is really going to go to work *for* him as well as its owner, and not be kept working to keep the poor poor just so long as the poor are satisfied to stay poor. Mere employment can no more be dangled before his worried artisan-eyes to keep him properly citified in poverty. Where now then is your poor man?

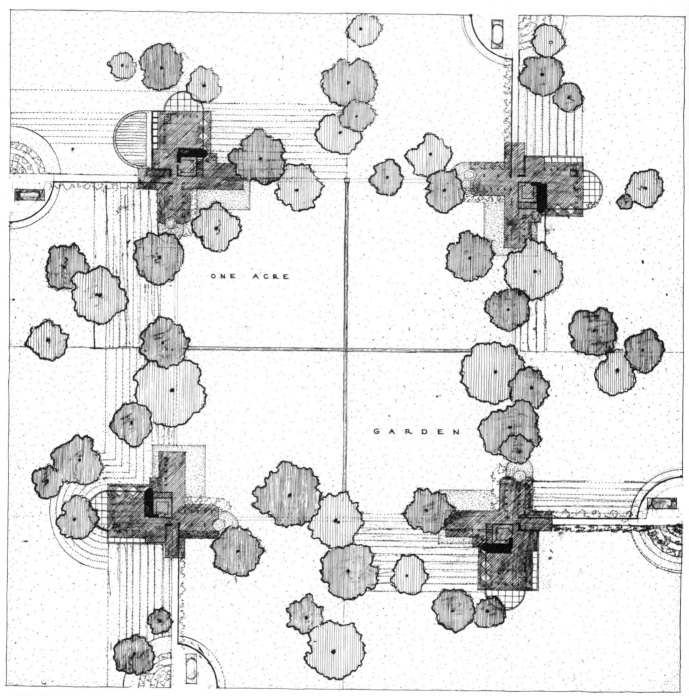

ONE ACRE

GARDEN

QUADRUPLE HOUSING, EXTERIOR PLAN

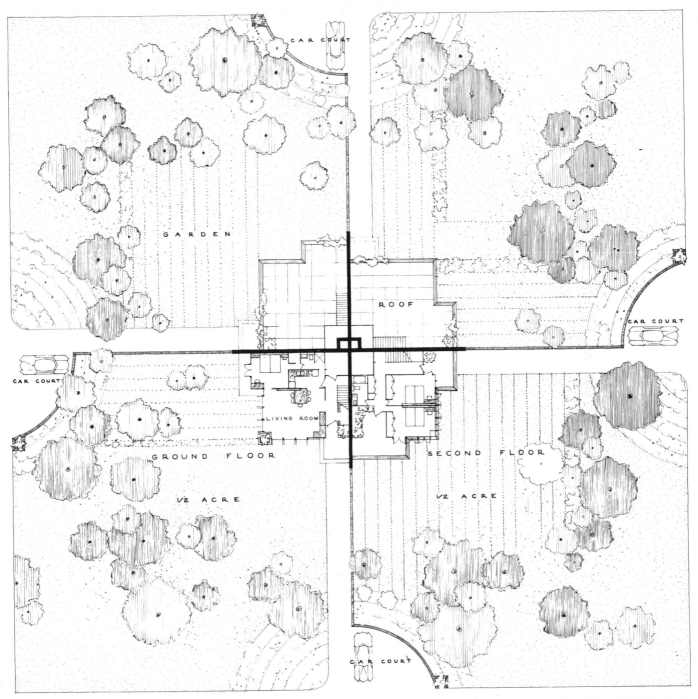

CAR COURT

GARDEN

ROOF

CAR COURT

CAR COURT

LIVING ROOM

GROUND FLOOR

SECOND FLOOR

1/2 ACRE

1/2 ACRE

CAR COURT

QUADRUPLE HOUSING, PLAN

Thus, in a year or two, "the poor" own a house at least home-worthy, staunch, and appropriate to inspiring environment. This home would be a house of real quality; one of a *great variety of such free houses* with good lines, good proportions, pleasant and "practical." Establishment would then be good to look at and as good to live in, because it would be well laid out according to ground; a garden in the prevailing generous ground-spacing. Such outbuildings as he might need—also appropriate standardized units—would be harmonious and would also be designed as extensions of his house itself. All together these would stand among shade trees, fruit trees, berry bushes, vegetables and flowers in the gardens. All houses would have hot and cold running water; a modern fireplace; electric cook-stove and electric heating system comprised in one single unit, bought and serviced by one single transaction. With some small aid in the way of social insurance (part of his new freedom) here is a quality home within reach of the artisan properly in the country by way of his compulsory devotion to the powers of the machine. Under these better, more co-operative conditions machinery could produce a good house for him more economically than his automobile. I mean the present horse-and-buggy car standing out there in a new fifty-dollar car-shelter, a part of his daily life until he can get a better one; at least a car designed for *him*. After all, it is time for us to waken to the fact that a modern car is neither a horse and buggy nor a ferry boat. Were electrification universal, as it will be, there would be cheap, standardized cars, just as standard light, heat, and power would be coming to him, underground, wherever he wanted to be. All cheap because of his voluntary co-operation with his neighbors; government imposed upon him only in those matters incapable of individuality—say police-powers. Such co-operation from government would simplify his circumstances and allow him to go nearer to life in many new ways without creating any more criminal conditions to be treated by government at his own expense.

Then, as a physical product—as things are—nothing is remarkable about extension to the poor of this opportunity. Taliesin was working upon this problem as early as 1921. The basis working underneath is already at hand. But remarkable is the fact that by way of organic design the whole establishment of the citizen may now have the kind of mass production that is inspired, and the kind of order that is "the first law of heaven." On no account need modern mass production lack the quality individuality alone can give if architects are truly architects. Choice as characteristic would belong to the citizen so freely that with appropriate design and practical devices available he could make his house a harmonious whole as appropriate to him as to his purse, to his ground as to his God. Where the workman has been thwarted by choice only of reactionary sentimentalities aborted by machinery, and compelled to accept ugly machine-made things put into a boxing-up by realtoristic bureaucracy, he will be equal in quality of investment to anyone "rich." The cottage has quality just as the mansion or factory or farm.

So, in the free city, where is your poor man? On a basis of equality he now has the same *quality* available to him as the rich. He can say his soul is his own because on his own ground opportunity has opened to him in natural ways. He has the right *to be*. Free to exercise his own faculties to the top of his bent, he becomes a gentleman because no longer enslaved to exercise himself as a soulless faculty of some machine-made producing system—probably for export! The erstwhile "poor" beside him are at least a block away, similarly situated on acreage of their own. Owing to genuine *quality* in design appropriate to time, place and circumstance he is at home related directly (and beautifully) to the ground he lives on and owns by improvement. He lives on his own in his own country: lives *with* the good ground *as a producer himself* not merely *on* it as a parasite of triple rent and hidden taxes. Birds sing for *him,* grass grows green for *him,* rain falls for *him* on his growing crops while the wheels of standardization and money-making invention no longer turn dead against him. All turn now *for* his majesty, the American citizen!

Are we ever to survive the ubiquitous Machine? If so it means increased life now to every man. Government, itself unaware always, must mean not only policing equal opportunity for all but be more concerned to improve the man. The machine is more the citizen's own concern—not government's —When Democracy Builds as it is surely going to do.

Is it too dangerous thus to allow the basis to exist for the free distribution of independence and liberty? Not in our country. This is the safest thing we as a people could do for our future: the really sane safe investment this

153

nation could make in itself and truly call our national "defense." No standing nation is minded to become a mere satellite. It could be always avoided and we could set the pattern for the world by rational *independence shared*: insure world peace—if we would. Peace? Invincible when based upon freedom such as this.

The Teen-Ager

The poor man's children growing up in the free city we see making first-hand contact with more of the freshness and sweetness of their birthright. Native ground and beauty any "rich" man's children now know. And this not by way of urban grass plots, nor as a goldfish, inhabiting a globe together with a pebble and a reed by sheer grace of some wife of a municipally minded landlord.

Once and for all he, "the poor man," as well as "the rich man," is now planted square with his fellows as spacious tillage grows more skillful by way of his work. He increases beauty of the countryside and it enriches all. Meantime, children so rationally educated know what the value of beauty, native, consists in; and by way of this new elemental education are taught to turn someday to teach the "ground" to the world.

In these new circumstances, individuality is thus likely to grow more mellow, gracious and true. Civilization bears better, not bitter, fruits, sane and shared by each and all citizens. A free city in a free nation. Aristocracy in the true democratic meaning of that misused word: aristocracy made integral: a genuine living *quality* instead of some dated hereditary privilege conferred by some dubious personal power.

To integrate general family small-garden and common little-farms production (to whatever extent this may be) and relate both to factory work and mental services a few hours each day; all the artifex is, and can produce, could be in so many ways economically related to the greater contact centers—extensive markets and factories standing there by the great highway; and rich resourceful neighborhood pleasure-places and civic centers; perhaps nearby as added feature are service-stations or wayside inns, the motels of the countryside.

154

This Broadacres family produce is regularly called for by men from these wayside markets, each day. Each day the *family* receives in cash one-half the value of whatever they can turn over to these collectors, whatever in its own free time in farmstead or in the shops elsewhere the family has raised and produced. And everyone now is where green-stuffs, produced fresh every hour, are commonplace. "Little-farms" thus reinforcing the larger, more expanded farm units would afford still greater variety of fresh produce to the city consumer, and some additional money would be earned by members of, say, the short-time machine-worker's own household: mother and children. Agrarianism holding its own; agronomy as cultural education for industrialism proceeds. Both could and would be co-operative. But as it now is, industrialism as producer is no fair partner for agronomy.

Where would the usual town-made employment be in the new circumstances? Nowhere. Where would the slums be? Nowhere. Abject poverty abolished. The teen-ager a valuable contributing factor. Integration of the various units by way of neighborhood kindergarten-schools, attractive travel everywhere, worthy entertainment, hospitals less needed and more humane, mutual insurance for sickness, accidents, the inabilities of old age; all these arranged to take from old-time machine-slaves the anxieties that bore them down to dump them into an early grave. Even were this start to be made as far down as the poorest of the poor, society would soon have self-respecting and respected creative individuals for citizens instead of increasing numbers of discouraged, bewildered alcoholics. And no such early retirement as now seems expedient. Instead of another cultural weed going to seed in urban municipal barracks all neatly lined up to raise more weeds indoors than outdoors, here we see a useful growing plant to sow more seeds of the healthy growing sort yielding a valuable mancrop for income. Good independent workmen would become more definitely a human asset. The workman nonetheless but the more a man because he happens to be the "machine age man." Even more a man because no longer a man-machine. He uses the machine too, yes, but the machine no longer uses him nor can it any longer abuse him. Yesterday he was only the machine "yes" man. Today, should he so choose, he is the "no" man or yes man—machine or no machine.

Life a Well-Calculated Risk

A democratic minor establishment (so far as it went) would be his. It would have potent charm, become a national *cultural* asset. Homes will be fit to be lived in with the pride of intelligent individuality. As the motorcar will someday come to look like a machine made fit for a human being to ride in, so organic in design, the house and car will look well together—can you imagine it? I can, and so will you although at present the automobile and the house are both out of scale, and utterly out of harmony with each other: the car an incongruous, foolish hangover—simply a commercialized exploit of the not sufficiently dim-and-distant-past until the new city begins on it and it begins on the new city.

All the various units of this artisan's new house could be built of native materials or fabricated of sheet-metal or composed of some form of composition-slab. Perhaps both together. Prefabrication here comes in as a natural. The house might be permanently built and "finished" like his car, in any texture or color he preferred but fit for a livable beautiful house. No "bad" color or unsuitable texture or pattern could be produced to be "preferred" in the new organic city because only good design is available. The house of the city-dweller might have much glass, but not enough to wither the tenant—glass screened from above by thin, sheltering wood or metal projections or shaded by the overhanging trellis hung with vines. Various units in one scheme might be wholly rectangular; in another hexagonal; another, circular in form. And all these not only laid out in plan projection but also in what *arises from the plan.* Thus infinite in variety, infinite combinations could be made of these elemental forms. A completed home unit might achieve the inclosure of a central court or garden with much greenery and flowers. Perhaps a pool. The establishment should grow as the trees around the man himself grow. He would be earning the natural increase due to the propensity of himself—his ability *to do* increased not merely because he is self-employed but because his own initiative is set free to employ himself and family in the greater advantage of other men like himself. Teen-age problems all disappear!

He could leave the roofs of his new dwelling flat and use them as a roof garden under awnings. Or, at some greater expense, he could slope the roof, protected by permanent materials, and use the ground around the house for recreation. Furnishings, throughout, like all appurtenance systems, would become a natural part of the house: good to look at inside as his house would be good to look at outside. Thus because he got his furnishings as he got his house: designed for him by the best talent the world affords, he might soon choose wisely for his own problem with a perfected knowledge? A range of choice now easily wide enough to enable the homemaker to find his own in his own way—with a proper feeling for nature.

Now the all-inspiring fact in this? The workman is in his free city on ground that cannot be taken away from him, because it is his, not by debt but by doing. That is to say, not his by signing away his sovereignty to any interest-bearing mortgage. It would be his own by way of good use and such appropriate improvements as he would himself make. There could be no landlord over him other than agreeable established social-superintendance given (he would need it and ask for it) by the cultivated society of which he would (in such circumstances) be a cultural unit himself. He would establish it. So the youth grows up an independent workman with ideas of his own which may find fruitful expression, because his education consists in what he does as he is actually learning to live on his own ground. Habitation not habituation is primarily his modern "liberal" education, based upon nature-study. His home is not only his own but naturally harmonious to the whole new city-scheme and environment. No longer is he some haphazard unit that must be officered by rank and file bureaucracy in an army of standardizations to which he was, once upon a time (and not so long ago), committed as "the poor." In all the free city there is no grim rent collected by fortuitous fortune or any other forms of success.

That is to say, here would be the manly family—men living in Usonia because all were privileged manlike in the freedom promised by democracy. Together with their own there is still much more than enough room for growth for everybody to come in, to come to America, her vast unused riches in ground to be well used.

Human independence and liberty fairly distributed where it belongs count most for our actual national defense. With the citizen protected by the character of his position and disposition—his conscience one of the best of assets—government would now truly represent him instead of being merely repressive. Government (and especially so) is his own affair—and again becomes the science of human happiness.

Optimistic, nonpolitical, ex-urban, vernal, spacious, free! All this—yes. In practical outline here is the feasible idea of organic social democratic reconstruction of the city belonging to creative Society—the living city. Abolish not only the "tenement" and wage-slavery but create true capitalism. The only possible capitalism if democracy has any future. True capitalism is not found under evasive practices necessary to maintain a plutocratic republic depending largely upon foreign trade for friendship and prosperity between nations—like a pyramid, apex on the ground, base in the air, maintained by artificial supports.

The Usonian Farmer—The Integration of the Family

For this farming citizen's share in our national life, what establishment would he, the farmer, have in Broadacre City?

Farmers now suffer from rent in its rankest, most virulent form. Any improvements the farmer makes are only a gamble adding to this burden of rent and probably ending somewhere down the line in foreclosure. Should his own labor be insufficient to pay rent for money, rent for land, and the rent exacted by far overgrown government, then goodbye to all his labor on farm improvement. The banker, as he takes over, takes his improvements. But in the free city, so long as he is able to work at all, he and his family can keep his land by his improvements and (by means of them) his own home where he made it, never fearing eviction. Poverty is thus far away from him if only he will work *at the work he likes* to do and knows best.

But farming at present is the hinterland of economics out there on the borderland of despair. Because the farmer was not taken into the present scheme of industrial or unearned increments, except as agronomy was gratuitous as a mere *source*. Intrinsic sources all become gratuitous too soon as factory-ized capitalized industry gains the upper hand. And in the more thickly settled regions of our country the farmer is still trying to compete against great grain-and-beef-raising by machine farming on the almost endless free acreage of our great, vast West. Grain-raising, as such, and beef are turning against him, and he must turn against both. Nor in cattle-and-sheep-raising can he well compete with these great ranges of western land held without need of improvement, taxed (if taxed at all) at a few cents per acre while the cost of the farmer's improvements always works dead against him on land taxed from fifteen to a hundred dollars (or more) per acre, plus taxed improvements.

Modern sanitation, motorcars, and electrifications like radio, television and flight, have brought the farmer's life a good deal nearer to the luxury of the sons and daughters of the prevailing white-collarite armies. But he is now (all too often) alone on his farm. And sometimes he is on the farm only to become an inmate of the poorhouse (would be better off if he were) at the end of his life's long labor on the ground, whatever may have been his energy and thrift—unless some tragic artificial stimulation such as war or government-spending comes to his rescue (for a short time only) eventually to push him deeper under when his turn comes to pay. This is his "relief."

Amusing or exasperating, as you may happen to take the view. See the empty political gestures his vote-getting saviors make to "relieve" him. He is the pawn in many a fulsome political game devised by false captains of urban fortune. Debt is forced upon the farmer as it is forced upon the wage-slave, for profit to what industrialism?

Despite these gestures made to "relieve" the farmer and the subtle subsidies offered him, not a statesman's voice is raised nor a single sensible legal move made to free him *fundamentally* from the inequalities that grip him for no other purpose than to give the white-collarite armies now serving industrialism a free ride on his back. These "volunteers" of our millions thus "citified" ride on the farmer's back to such an extent because the farmer's labor is *intrinsic*. It is a Source. A source is always infested by the petty parasites of the big parasite in our thriving era of the Middleman: the salesman. The farmer's labor on land contributes chiefly to maintain the characteristic vicarious powers of crowded city life: powers growing more than ever vicarious; power by lever and pushbutton help him on the one hand and push him back on the other. But the farmer's labor does not contribute very much beyond food and privations to his own life except as gratuities. Parasites are parasitic because they must and (it is *no* fault of theirs) batten upon innocent sources of production; live upon *origins:* doomed never to live by originating. So here in our own tiller of the soil is good and genuine life in deep trouble. By way of the preferred parasitism and paraphernalia of our continually increasing mechanical centralization we have to fake our capitalism. Unless the farmer turns and exploits centralization instead of being exploited by it, he is down to stay down for a long time.

Ground is seldom his own ground except as he holds it like his machinery by some slender show of "equity." The farmer—East, Middle West, or South —is no winner of the game of increments as that game is played, for high stakes with the rules of money-getting now established as a kind of betting-game. The financial dice are loaded against him by the very circumstances in which they are held and he is placed. He will "find" himself in time as and if he can, but only in a city like Broadacres.

The Great Mouth

Cities are huge mouths. Essentially the farmer is food-master for the great mouth. He has many subsidiaries, but his primary job is to feed these great feudal survivals of the city. Raw materials for clothing himself and the urbanites are still his job. Without the farmer our towns and cities, big and small, would go naked and starve.

But in the new free city he himself comes in for a due place and share. The new city will go out to service him as he services the city, the citizen not merely there to be fed but to share in the common luxury which the very nature of the farmer's intrinsic service to society has now made possible—bounty hitherto denied the farmer. Society will share indigenous culture with the farmer. His establishment is now most welcome to all as a fine feature of the city. His will be, perhaps, the most attractive establishment of all the structures of the new freedom.

For feeding the multitude, naturally the farmer's job, it is clear that intensive farming, varied as possible, will be a great social advantage. The vast western grain- and beef-producing areas will no longer compete with him. Instead of there being no place for him—he will take their place. One great

160

advantage the citizen has: his produce, at last, will be direct from producer to consumer. The ubiquitous middleman, too often now a "Sinbad the sailor," will be off the farmer's back. Dairying, fruit-growing, truck-gardening, raising the rarer meats, fowl, eggs, in all of which freshness is a first consideration, will be the direct contribution of society to itself. The tin can and barbed wire fence, once upon a time the bulwarks of advancing western civilization, are gone. He is himself no longer fenced in, or tangled up in his own barbed wire by ubiquitous, inglorious debt. Agronomy, the equal of industrialism or superior, is the gifted source of our national culture—even now—if you take a fair view at our country.

As the natural agronomy we are describing proceeds, there will be a new farmer and his family in Broadacres. He will, by intensive methods, gradually take the place of the "dirt" farmer and his family of pioneer days.

The little-farms farmer—or his farmsters and farmerettes—will need a greenhouse; need less than one small portion of the land he tried to farm before he became a Usonian citizen. As a citizen he now needs a completely fireproof sanitary establishment, one that makes his lifework more pleasant, and a charming association with the higher-grade animals he husbands— breeding, feeding and tending them, primarily doing so for the new city, for the millions who meantime have cultivated their tastes, no longer their idiot-syncrasies, let us say. Or, let us say, cultivated increased knowledge rather than taste. Before everything else the new farmer will now need most (and know best) the nature-study we call organic architecture. He will need the kind of buildings now that will end unceasing tramping in mud or snow in and around about the ill-smelling inefficient group of ill-adapted buildings that had become a habit to him and a disgrace to his country. Organic design is able to supplant them all with one compact, well-correlated, fireproof, prefabricated building efficient for his every purpose, a vermin-proof building that considers his own life on the farm worthy of conservation and culture. The little-farms farmer's dignity, living comforts and cultural education of his children, as organic, are assured. He needs less but has much and more in almost every way worthwhile than when he thought by big acreage he too was "big." He no longer needs big areas, big machines or a multiplicity of sheds. Out-buildings of any kind would muss up his place. But he does need an intimate workshop and modern tools. He does not any more need many fences except those a part of his buildings or electrified boundary lines.

His energy is conserved by having all these conveniences together now under one convenient, sanitary, fireproof, model building; his animals a few steps away approached under cover; his motorcar or small truck reached by opening the door from his dwelling to a garage; his crop prescribed and sold, even before he raises it, by some plan of integration with larger or smaller little-farms markets. This market itself would be a comprehensive scheme for the integration of the many small farm units into greater uses, making available to them the choicest products of the world in art, literature or science. This integration, being inevitable, is destined to take the place of devastating back-and-forth haul of produce and of humanity itself in the present overgrown centralizations of all our big cities and even small towns. Distributions become everywhere direct. From factory and farm to family becomes more than a mere slogan.

This composite farm-building would be made up of assembled prefabricated units. Shelter for cars, a comfortable dwelling, greenhouse, a packing and distributing place, silo (narrow and tall or short and wide), stables for cows and horses, and diversified animal shed for sheep, pigs, etc. The whole establishment would be good architecture. Good to look at. Emancipation for the life of the farmer. As such the whole farm-unit could well be delivered to the farmers at low cost by machine production intelligently expanded and standardized. For the first time organic architecture would become his own, serving him by way of the best brains utilized to simplify and make his life more dignified and his whole family effective help. Their life would become attractive not only to themselves but to the new city itself, a feature of a true modern agronomy countrywide.

This composite little-farms building would be a group building not of one type only as here shown but of as many types in various materials as there are bound to be endless modifications of the farmer's purposes and his ground—or as seen now in our better buildings of more affluent citizens.

This architectural modernization of the very *basis* of all good farming would be a most important phase of "farm relief"—after the freedom of man, land and money is once established in normal channels for building a genuine American culture as a great beneficent agronomy.

162

Well-designed farm life grouped thus on units of five- ten- or forty-acre farms (or more)—production prescribed, or not—all buildings and equipment designed directly related to highway traffic and supermarkets selling farm produce fresh hourly—this is much more than mere "farm relief." It is true functioning on the broad basis of any democratic economy radical to our vast gift of magnificent ground.

Also of great importance is the design of the little-farms markets themselves. Additional festive social feature—these markets—of urban integration among the many minor service features found along the interior roadways of the highways of the free city.

A single tractor held in common could spread the tilth, power the disk, and harrow the soil for many farmers. Group ownership could be common, and the various community centers of various districts (now called county seats) could provide not only power distribution but pooling of certain labors and interests in case of sickness, or an economy in health. But also community-provided would be varied social entertainments, all of increasingly superior cultural character. Seasonal festivity of great inspirational value for all? All the races involved would soon be contributing to common neighborhood events in terms of the unifying intercommunications by air Today, far beyond those of Yesterday.

Here in suggestive outline only is organic "farm relief" and urban release. A happier, fuller livelihood for so many millions of uneasy white-collarites —become capable as free men and women—not quite happy as city-parasites wrestling with a teenager problem. By further subdivision and reintegration of smaller units, enabling upbuilding of general living conditions on a stronger basis, millions of our citizens would find the means of life that would be defense against propaganda, political oppression—or plain boredom. Population an asset not a threat. Quality would become the ideal. Citizenship no longer compelled to rent the chattels of any cash-and-carry system whatsoever! They would be citizen-owners of themselves.

So in every single county section of Broadacre City there would be plenty of room for the many varied occupations each integrated with all and independent. The superfluous millions of white-collarites now forever seeking and abandoning employment in the old cities would be happy independents in a beautiful life in beautiful country.

No, "employment" is not enough! What a man wants, if democracy works, is not so much employment as freedom to work at what he believes in, what he likes to do. Officially dangling employment before a man now may be, after all, only the means of keeping him tied to a form of slavery—now some money-getting or money-distributing system that amounts to some form of conscription when any showdown comes. "Full-time employment" in the new city might cast the same shadow-of-doubt on man's future economic life as it did in the old. The nature of leisure will be more integrated with the nature of work than ever; work and leisure become natural to each other.

"Business" and Architecture

To say that "business" will some day know good architecture suited to its purpose before art, science, education and religion are able to recognize it, may be astonishing but I believe, nevertheless, true. Perhaps this recognition by business is not so much perception of the eternal fitness of things as it is again the flair for the best new expedient or what is "good advertising."

It would seem however that good business *is* heading in toward good architecture? The manufacturer, world over, in this has been leader. Perhaps this because "culture," in quotation marks, had no place for it but in the final decisions of business—the mind of the superior businessman was more free than the pseudo-cultural academic to accept the change that is progress.

INDUSTRIALIZATION

The Factory

The factory?

A factory comes naturally enough to our countrywide countryside city. Government employees themselves become, more and more, small-farms gardeners. The factory is already so well organized, built, and managed that it needs less redesigning than any enterprising unit we have. But it

164

needs more ground free; more space available for decentralization; also much ground free to the factory workers. The big factory will subdivide, soon recognize the need for dividing itself up into smaller units spaced according to the new standards of space measurement largely due to the car: more economic freedom for the worker in order to make him a purchaser as well as a producer. Broadacre reintegration is division of the big factory into smaller units based upon events already taking place in many great industries. Factories will be first to see and help put an end to absurd waste motion. The factory, except for exaggeration of size due to overcentralization and the imprisoning of factory workers in "housing," is the best thing America has yet done. Great improvement on English precedents, our new varied factories are the most socially important units we have yet accomplished—not far, now, from ready to subdivide and reintegrate as the more desirable and sightly features of our new free city.

Business Offices

Commercial office buildings?

The financial, professional, distributive, administrative business edifice may be where it would naturally belong, to function as a unit of whatever business it might serve. Instantaneous intercommunication by air makes a return direct to origins not only good business, not only a desirable life-saver, but *reasonable*. Practical. The only good "business." Movement has started, and correlation of offices, manufactures, farming, with dwelling, will become more and more desirable; and is more and more going to the country. The commodity belt has less and less chance of survival. Why not accomplish this by good planning rather than let it happen haphazard? Efficient conservation of time and energy by the worker, the manufacturer and the farmer (all as co-operating citizens) will benefit producer and consumer alike. Much easier to work continuously forward from the plant than it ever was to work continually forward to and backward from it as in the circumstances of life in the present to-and-fro.

And offices for public officialism, petty or major (bureaucracy such as might still remain above ground) could center in police and fire stations now at present county seats. Already existing county seats would nearly all be at natural road junctions, but, owing to lack of congestion, villages might be cut down to one out of the two or three operating now at waste expense, and certain parts of all the establishments be planted to trees or grass. District courts of law—greatly reduced by the simplifications of a true "people's government"—would also be found at this point, functionaries and functioneers established there beside them. None would be found in braggadocio buildings, the exaggerations now customary, because such official functions are really not grand but merely *utilitarian*. So Michelangelo's dome and its myriad offspring, the cupola, column and pilaster, the paraphernalia of the classic, would vanish with the ostentatious facades. Architraves and cornices out of luck.

The Professional

Offices of the many kinds and kindred of professional men would be especially built for their work and be found usually in connection with their own home grounds. Or be interesting minor features of the new city. Various edifices for professionals might be set up, but "professionalism" would diminish, wherever recognized as a depreciation of form, regarded as gangsterism properly refined. Many small shops, or call them studios, clinics, small hospitals or art galleries, suited to "professional" purposes, would be found usually semidetached from the dwelling places. "Show-off" places too would be designed for any purpose whenever desired as machine age luxury. Such highly individualized professional units and the shops of all kinds of specialists, added to the homes, would enrich and variegate the aspects of the new city, save us from the battle of the sign-boards and, again, from all the enormous waste of the old back-and-forth haul of the professional from his suburb to his city.

Professional services would have a chance to become better and more economical as they were directly available to patients or clients under the convenient conditions that would characterize Broadacres. Also professionals would be easier to reach than through the traffic hindrances of present centralization which does violence to both time and nerves of both patient and doctor. The professional man of today needs less wear-and-tear on the man, more time for service, research, and creative study of nature in an inspiring atmosphere.

166

Bank, Banker and Banking

The bank?

Oh, well, banks (money marts) should be found with other official buildings at some county seat or important road junction. Banks should be seen as integrated units in strong social credit systems. So the bank need no longer put on the airs of a temple of worship or any place of divinity. Service would be integrated with the social system. No need to hold up importance further with columns or a "front" to get business preferences from depositors. Bank credits financing production for use would have no money except as a demurrage currency having no commodity value in itself whatever. The credit of the People would therefore be in their own hands without unfair exploitation by broker or any system of interlocking insurance—the banker an integrated, dedicated member of his society.

So a "bank" would be only a well calculated responsibility, not of the individual but of the people! A nonpolitical, non-profit institution in charge of medium of exchange—a medium having, in itself, no possible speculative value. A bank therefore might have its own character as would a good, dignified filling station or church. Grandomania in construction, as seen in bank buildings themselves, great cut stone quarries for offices, enormous safes and locks appealing to superstitious depositors, would no longer be needed for prestige. Money itself as a power would no longer be glamorized; and be no direct invitation to thievery. These temples-of-unearned-increment would shrink to an open office somewhere for the more intrinsic uses of more intrinsic money—a mere medium of exchange. Credits instead of hard cash would be all the bank would contain. The enterprise of the bank-robber would be gone. But—what about an international standard of value for our rich production bosses? Consult Social Credit! The most practical of all the systems of "money" or foreign-exchange yet devised, because based upon the self-contained independence of each and every nation's citizenry.

Markets

Great spacious roadside pleasure places these markets, rising wide and handsome like some flexible form of pavilion—designed as places of co-operative exchange, not only of commodities but of cultural facilities. "Business" takes on a different character: integration of mercantile presentation and distribution of all produce possible and natural to the living city. These markets might resemble our county fairs, in general, and occur conveniently upon great arteries of mobility. These fine features of the future are already appearing in embryo. Even if neglected and despised, they are fingers pointing the end of centralism. Already appearing like roadside service stations, they are probably the beginning of future collateral cultural centers directly established and owned by the people.

In our present gasoline service station you may see a crude beginning of such important advance decentralization; also see the beginning of the future humane establishments we are now calling the free city.

Wherever service stations are located naturally, these now so often ugly and seemingly insignificant features will survive and expand into various important distributing centers of all sorts. They are already so expanding in the great Southwest. Each of these smaller service units might be again integrated or systematically "chained" in a series over large areas, to down costs and facilitate distribution; add new economies to production and standardizing of other products besides gasoline. Such widespread centers of distribution would become general distributors of many things that Marshall Field, Sears Roebuck, Montgomery Ward or Wanamaker now distribute by mail to the congested crowds senselessly swarming in from the country to hard pavements and back again.

Most important—fresh opportunity for building by the people themselves is everywhere found in this diversified wayside market and its tributaries. A daylight store in a park, it would be perhaps the most attractive, educational and entertaining single modern unit to be found among all new features. Parking facilities generous, adequate self- or service-parking, none now seem to realize how extensive this will be. Easily accessible room in the city will be everywhere for beguiling entertainments. Open-air concerts, cabarets, cafes, the theatre. Restaurants—good—with charm will be found at roadsides and at the markets as they will be found at roadside service stations. In certain places nearby, the luxury motel for overnight accommodation of transients will appear more and more, making continuous travel a delightful, comfortable experience. A cultural affair—this motel? Yes, and competition between various centers would develop, and individuality determine success or failure. Soon, from any and every traffic stream, one will turn aside into charming places not imitating those of any country to pick up in the *natural to-and-fro* of everyday traffic all or anything needed or desired at home. To deprive the age not too suddenly of its characteristic art of outdoor advertising, prospective purchasers might be subjected to the same temptations by effective sales displays such as now entertain and amaze in any of our highly specialized stores, but this advertising to be "built in"—never "roadside." Advertising would be concentrated, designed or incorporated as features of each particular building—the market. Proprietors, as salesmen or managers, all would be living not too far away. Not far away, now, is within ten or twenty-five miles: living in country places of their own choosing. Children would be going to nearby Broadacre country schools. "Nearby" being within miles, now, instead of a few city blocks. Citizens themselves would more likely be the improved modern equivalent of ancient landed gentry? The democratic artistocracy of a great democracy.

The Realtor

In all these various evaluations of establishment we have made, we have had time to see only a few changes for the better by better uses of our machine power—power at present only working to multiply in deadly fashion what goes to work *on,* instead of *for* creative humanity. If throughout the new Usonian social fabric we would courageously *plan* in the light of the law of natural change, as, say, Marshall Field followed it when establishing stores in big city outskirts and many small towns; as Woolworth and his followers have followed; then that would be an indication of the free city of democracy coming along—no longer haphazard but organic. So, ahead of the pioneer centralizations of yesterday by the big realtor operating to accommodate the gregarious instinct of humanity, there naturally arises the next step: pioneering by decentralization. The urbanizing realtor in the discard. Tomorrow would bring along with it the social reintegration that establishes, defends and insures greater human happiness. Port towns and such localities as are near concentrations of natural materials would be subject to concentration as a matter of nature. But all this ends in most big and little inland towns.

Modern invention and machine resources, increasing the destructive interferences to human life in present cities and towns, not only compel the point of view taken here for the future (if we are to have a future) but they are already compelling unwilling citizenry to take heed and consider "moving out." As best it may, the present "system" is concealing from itself the very nature of what is now happening to destroy the makeshift eventually.

Apartments

As for the apartment building, whether tall, big or small, perhaps it, too, could go to the country for another lease of life. Certainly so for the early time being. This now disturbing tall building in shadow, crowding its own shadow, and gathering and emptying its crowds on city streets might be one of the very first steps toward urban rescue—become exurban as infirmary for the sidewalk-happy citizen. The tall building in such circumstances might be similar to the one proposed for an apartment tower in the small park of St. Mark's-in-the-Bouwerie in New York City, first designed 1921, and built as the Price Tower in Bartlesville, Oklahoma, 1955.

This arrangement (in quadruple) of indestructible airy duplex apartments is built and furnished complete. Such luxury apartments would stand in small parks, say several acres more or less, with particularly easy accommodation for parking dwellers' cars beneath the ground floor level— out of sight. Playgrounds and small gardens for each tenant would be alongside on the ground level as features of the small park enabling beneficent absorption into the countryside as a feature of education of the too many children of too many unqualified parents.

Such structures would enable many people who have grown so accustomed to apartment life to go to the country under highly serviced conditions if unwilling or unable (it is much the same thing) to establish themselves in the free city.

170

Towers of prismatic metals; steel, concrete and glass; shafts rising above greenery, each on its own private green, would be acceptable to Broadacres. Advantages of the countryside—fresh air, beautiful views, freedom from noise and the traffic jam, growing acquaintance with nature—could all well go to occupants of these tall buildings. And each in-dweller might own his apartment. Own it on the improved economic terms of the life he would be living: now able to turn the key on his abode and travel without great risk or sacrifice. Also there is the plan of the quadruple—in quadrangular array—widespread and beneficent—instead of the standardized subdivision based upon the ancient London dormitory town.

Motels

As a matter of course there would be few or no hotels in their present commercial sense. Now a bad feature of the overconcentration of the city, they are already disappearing in favor of the luxury motel. Each motel, now as hotel, would probably be a group of small units conveniently related to a larger unit comprising public services—separate rooms for use of all guests, as already seen in the better planned motel. And establishments like the Arizona Biltmore, or San Marcos in the desert designed for Chandler, Arizona, would serve as resorts for tired millionaires. These hostelries would probably be found where Nature stages a beautiful show in which they could be well employed for recreation and recuperation. All hangovers from the old city life, especially "the tired businessman," could be humanely cared for without destroying too much.

The motel is a comparatively new manifestation of American life. Better suited to urbanite survivals would be the mobile hotel itself "going places" on wheels. Made for the purpose of the transient to go to universally famous scenic regions; fully equipped to keep house.

These new free wheeling mobilites would be commodious, with sleeping accommodations, touring the country, with cuisine abroad. They would cruise North to South or East to West, stop awhile at places of unique charm or interest, places inaccessible otherwise because of short seasons or practical inaccessibility. And also there is the inflatable home thrown into the back of the car and blown to size at the site.

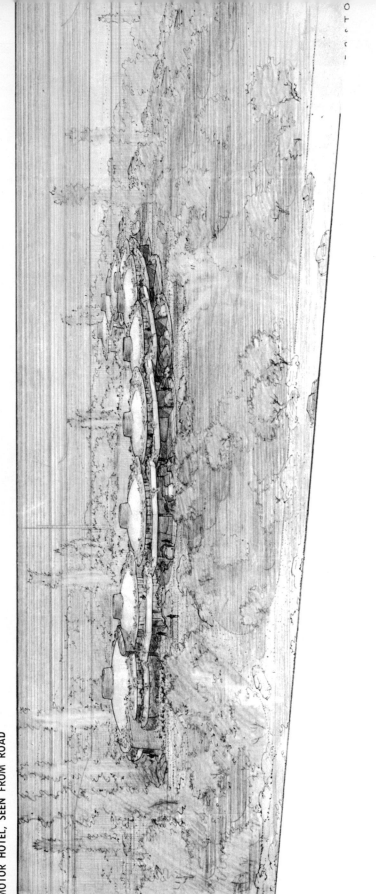

MOTOR HOTEL, SEEN FROM ROAD

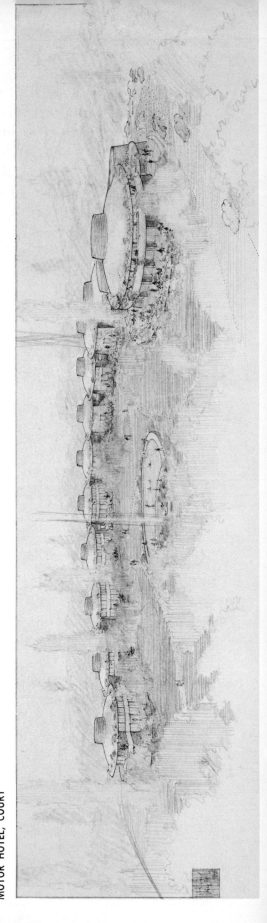

MOTOR HOTEL, COURT

MOTOR HOTEL, PLAN

Various attendant trailers, trains attractive in design, suitable lorries, and the mobile house, would be found along highways leading to great plains or mountain ranges. They could go where no other hostelry could be and survive.

Insomuch as the comfortable nature of transport is steadily developing everywhere, there is little reason why such mobile motels and hotels should not be beautiful as well as mobile, profitable and comfortable. Some such form was developed by the McArthur brothers at Phoenix, Arizona, 1927, and intended to be a feature of the Arizona Biltmore Hotel. If these fantastic schemes are feasible for use as branches of prominent hotels, why not also feasible as a dwelling place? Without picturesque disaster if well designed.

Mobility might apply to the lakes and streams themselves by way of charming motorized houseboats radio-equipped, serviced regularly by small boats from shore, each and all designed as appropriate features charming in the waterscape as well designed cottages could be in our native landscape—like the Lake Tahoe project in 1922.

Pleasure-seekers, employers, employees, explorers, artists, artisans (and wise men) all could have these road-traveling ships or floating barges at moderate cost. All live in them with convenience. The modern gypsies? Facilities for superlative design could make them as desirable at least as any plane or car.

At a householder's will, his motor house or motor barge could go about from place to place, linger at mountain lake or resorts otherwise inaccessible to him—or upon suitable rivers and lakes—as the nomad once upon a time drifted over the desert with his camel and his tent. Under proper control this type of total mobility might be added to Usonian life.

Community Centers

The community center would also mean more because it would be salient feature of every countryside development of the county, wherever the county seat might be. The civic center would always be an attractive automobile objective—perhaps situated just off some major highway in interesting landscape—noble and inspiring.

BARGE, "FALLEN LEAF"

BARGE FOR TWO

Golf courses, race tracks, the zoo, aquarium, planetarium—all would be found at this general Center. Good buildings grouped in architectural ensemble with botanical gardens, art museum, libraries, galleries, opera, etc.

There might also be suitable country clubs nearby. But the community center would be the great common club of clubs, avoiding commonplace elegance and overcoming popular prejudice of town partisanship. The community center, liberal and inspiring, would be a general culture-factor because it would be an entertainment center. The art gallery a popular rendezvous, not so much a museum; a "morgue" no longer. Both grounds and buildings of the various centers would be gradually developed in harmony with one another so that each center might take on its own charm and individuality; therefore, why not itself be a great work of art? Scattered over the states, placed at various county seats of each, the community center thus would catch, retain, and express the best thought of which growing American democracy is capable. Commercial bustle and competitive humdrum or humbug diminished. The community center a respected, respectful place—a place for quiet comradeship suited to inspection, introspection and good company concerning both people and things.

THE NEW THEATRE

The New Theater

Wherever a phase of Nature will have been raised by society to the level of greater Nature there we will find the Theater and find the people themselves owner and producer. Theater would be radical, arousing, inspiring, challenging popular emotion, presenting native problems. Human strength and aspiration would go there for inspiration. The theater would be no old soap-box either—no, and the old peep-show would be gone. With new opportunity to present life, no longer would scenes be enacted behind a proscenium and seen through this hole in the wall. The theater would be no circumstance as in the days of its origin. The stage itself would be cycloramic and, if needed, panoramic, more and more an automatic machine

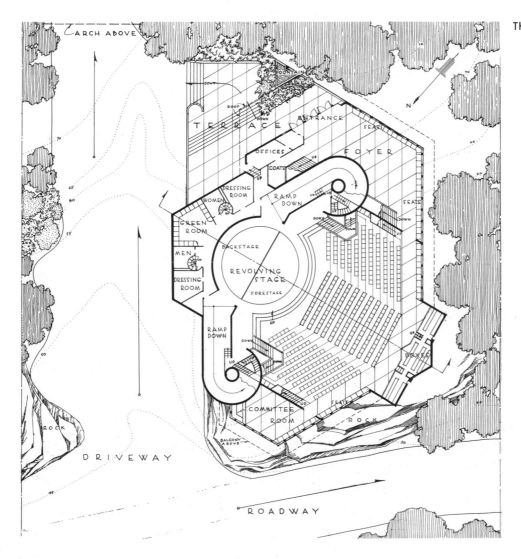

THE NEW THEATRE, PLAN

that would endow the theater with the plasticity the cinema has already taken to itself. The architecture of this feature of the developed civic center would probably be placed underground, worked out by artists in the new movements built by new uses of plasticity. Inhabitants of the whole county would probably often become performers themselves in preference to employed entertainers. The present star-system would gradually be abolished? But traveling "stars" or companies would be welcome on occasion if the occasion (or the star) survived and was changed by the changed circumstances.

Where desired by the homemaker, cinema, like the theater, taken from the marketeer and having the people now for producer (or sponsor), would go from original source into every home and public place. Entertainment both as sound and vision would become something freely, freshly imaginative, well executed; and cinema and tape recordings, continuously distributed by subscription, would be in the circulating libraries. No censorship but public opinion. At every community center there would be a continuous series of especially important features both in theater and cinema. All such would be *maintained by the community itself*—and liberally. None such would any longer be left to the mercy of any salesmanship for big production nor of any monopolizing commercial element whatever; nor ever again be used as a sales agency to put the nation into war or the huckster into the parlor, or the gangster into the bedroom. Nor could any secret salesmen, molders or soldiers of public opinion (hirelings themselves), ever reach the public for any such purpose.

Great music would mean something to be widely distributed to the people. The radio not dead but more alive than ever. Like the cinema, music would become the vital cultural affair it is—a cultural feature of the Usonian family at home, alongside architecture. The chamber music concert would naturally become a common feature at home; players growing up until it amounted to a home culture beyond mere entertainment. No uncommon accomplishment for children to learn to read music readily, play the piano and some other instrument as well. Music universal—like the culture of music in the old days of the family concerts à la recorder—may come alive again. The piano alone is enough. Knowledge of good music and reading it in score should be as universal a practice as reading books or the funnies; as essential as the reading of plans by the architect or reading the stars. And the reading of plans should be as universal an accomplishment as the reading of print.

The Light That Failed

The Church. Why does the church no longer lead man out of merchant-dom into realms of the poetic principle? Why should it attempt to follow the merchant and so become itself a merchant? Is this because the church is essentially unsuited to the sovereignty of the individual, being by nature some form of submission to opinion by hierarchy? Not freedom? Not Nature? Not Jesus nor the great philosophers who were like Him? And why not?

Was that why Jesus opposed the establishments called churches? Could abnegation of the Spirit in order to keep on good terms with the prevailing practices of the profit-motive in this machine age possibly withstand the revelations now made by science, and curb the curiosity aroused by the growing universal tides of sophisticated intelligence?

"Revelations" by science can be only partial. But the organized religion of the Church, too, seems as of now even more partial. The Church, as it was and still is, can never thrive in our spirit of individual democracy—the machine age—the age of the merchant. Certainly not in the democracy in this new city of the future. In that city the church, too, will change, become more integral, a deeper student of human nature.

Honest compromise between the ideal of success according to present merchantable money-getting systems and a true Religion is no longer likely. Is it because compromise after compromise in the interest of universal compromise has been attempted and failed, that the old idea of church, like the old idea of a city, is now hopelessly dated? Subject to change the church will grow more genuinely democratic in spirit; less and less sectarian; more liberal in thought therefore more comprehending of men and their faith in themselves as men; less concerned with the hereafter, with livelihood and deference to authority; less a sectarian institution which, though based upon humility, allows partisanship, prejudice, and superstition to live nevertheless; and understanding the difference between selfishness and selfhood. Democracy in the new city will want religion back in its true place. That place Jesus prophesied will be high up indeed. Probably higher than ever before. Never merchantable.

Church Building

Church architecture, like most college architecture, has been false to its opportunities. This for a century at least. The Church of Democracy—tomorrow no feudal survival—is finding for itself a true new form. It will be organic building more suitable to modern feeling for the sincere sentiment of worship. Education, too, when cultural in our democracy, will find the kind of building more suitable to its actual office than imitations of Oxford Gothic or anything else it has imitated.

Traditional church forms, like so many traditions now, must die in all minor forms in order that Tradition in great form may live! To understand this truth is to understand the changing growth that is already due to the idea of democracy, and to make way for the return of worship to the life of the citizen as well as for the uplift and integrity the nation requires to endure. As Walt Whitman and Emerson and Thomas Jefferson prophesied.

True religion never dies, because indispensable to man's life as well as his work. But, since the last great war, the Church, as we knew it then, must be buried. Deep.

True religion? Assuming religious sentiment would have had opportunity and occasion to survive the sidewalk-happy Broadway mind, it might deepen in the urban citizen's breast a reassuring living faith in man. Assuming that the falsity of the old sentimentalities of the fashionmonger would have diminished, the falsity as oppressive to the popular spirit in an enlightened democracy as it always should have been to the church; assuming the church would have survived in spite of the multiplicity of competitive churches, it would be likely to take nonsectarian form; more spiritual; more devotional; combining intellectual vision (the brilliant light of the West) with a softer, more earth-loving and deeper feeling for nature (the glowing light of the East). Here would be another great opportunity—perhaps the greatest of all—for the expression of true religion—religion a great human synthesis seen again as great architecture. So the church, by

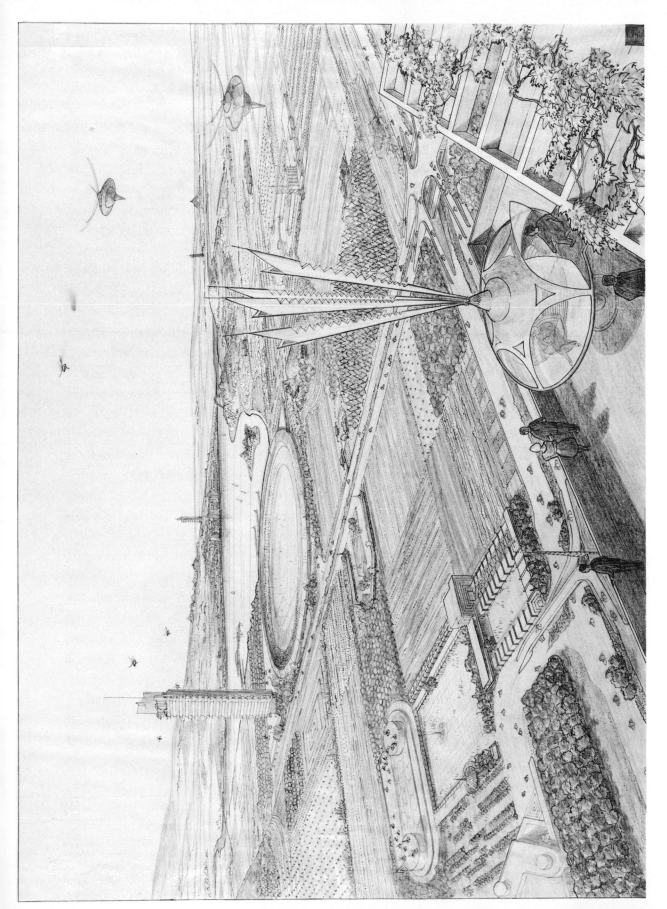

TYPICAL VIEW OF BROADACRES COUNTRYSIDE. PATTERNS OF CULTIVATION MINGLING WITH GOOD BUILDINGS. HELICOPTER SEEN IN FOREGROUND AND, BEYOND, AUTOMATIC OVERPASS ENABLING CONTINUOUS, UNINTERRUPTED TRAFFIC FOUR WAYS

way of the ideal building in the free city, might be as a song without words, comprising minor churches grouped about a common meeting place. It is certain, in any case, that the new church would be a rendezvous with the very heart of great Nature. Thus will be served the depths and breadths of the universal spirit belonging to democracy. Church will again become the citizen's haven of refuge and he no less individual in his chosen terms of worship but more profound and comprehensive.

In these days of the commercial merchandising of humanity, regardless, spiritual degeneracy falls upon the youth of the world; the teenager problems increase. The church has sought to administer partisanship, conscription, and what is called "public opinion" in these pragmatic days of the modern materialist; the fomentation of war. But the over-all harmony of this new city might arise, and shine again, as the way of the church? Architecture could serve again to restore or refresh the mortal weariness brought by our foolish "success"—in the church itself, in our private lives, our commerce, our Congress. We have been amused by the wily cynic in this rancid era of the machine. In our ultra servility to the pessimism of this machine age, we all need the recreation found only in exercise of faith, free man's faith in man himself, faith in our new human privilege—our Democracy—faith kept and renewed by honest work for our great ideal of freedom. Theology can never again teach advocates of such faith, nor be anything more than troublesome pettifoggery. Our Broadacre City church, then, would be another Cathedral, unhistorical edifice for the fusion of all that is best in all the historical religions; it would be the greatest single wonder in the architecture of Broadacre City. Worship there would again be universal practice, protected once more in modern times by and for the free spirit of individual man. Here at last would be a great church not built by individuals separate, but by all the creeds together in order to promote—in terms of a tempered and well directed machine age culture, organic—a finer sensibility concerning what it is that constitutes a growing man's well-being in our time. Religion should thus promote firmer faith in the nobility and beauty of which human nature is divinely capable when once made truly free from within. In Broadacres the Cathedral could become again, and upon more noble social terms, the potent cultivator of independence, protector of the neighbor, pilot of human conscience, and

182

thus alive for a whole people. Church would have no quarrel with science, science no quarrel with art, because science would need this church, and art, again great, would understand (as, indeed, would philosophy) that the true Art and Science of man are from within and that without them the life of no man is free.

The Hospital

The present hospital, efficient and humane as it is, but seldom, is now usually much too large—and growing larger. Through no fault of its own, the hospital has fallen to the obvious stature of a great business institution, but Broadacre hospitals would be sanatoriums of many types. Sunlit clinics connected together in natural ways or by artfully made park-like fountain-gardens, each building especially planned for individual privacy instead of the much too much generality and promiscuity of the usual hospital. Homelike residence would be so arranged in them (and of them) that no disabled or sick person need see another disabled or sick person (patient) unless either so willed. Resources of modern therapy, surgery, and medicine would be in their places, just as the plumbing, electric lighting, and heating would be; none visible as fixtures or features.

In short, emphasis in the new hospital would be on normality, not on the paraphernalia of abnormality. Death's head continually shows in the present-day hospital. Why is the hospital not as humanely practical in aesthetic effect as it tries to be in physical purpose? And yet our hospitals are among the most effective and well managed units found in cities. But in Broadacres hospital-service would be rendered to the people by the people. At any cost? No. Free.

Education and Culture

"The soul without knowledge is without power." But without right practice too the soul is likely to fester?

Can that "soul" be considered educated who cannot read drawings? Cannot read the plan-documents that make everything made for man or around about him—the drawings, plans and details? Yes, fundamental plan-reading should begin early in our education because essential to all for understanding the constructions of life. The Friedrich Froebel kindergarten method for the development of creative children is the most needed element as antidote to the play sentimentalities of the present kindergarten system.

Should a man be considered educated, knowing nothing of the properties of line and color or the chemistry of good design, nothing of what constitutes a good building, knowing nothing about plants or the nature of the food he puts into his mouth or *the nature* of his own bodily functioning? Is that man "educated" knowing little or nothing of his real self, of the underlying principles of structure or aesthetics as well as the dynamics of *form*? When form and color, so essential to architecture, are left to the mercy of "taste," the soul is like some rudderless ship sailing uncharted seas. The science and especially the art of structure is basic to all true human culture. When education is without this foundation, it is a liability, not an asset.

Should that man be considered educated who knows nothing of the cosmic rhythms of sun, moon, and stars elemental in art, nothing of the effect they have upon *him* in whatever he does, in his dreaming, planning, planting, reaping, or breeding; his dancing, singing, or building?

Well, until the groundwork of his education is acquired from interior Nature, do not speak of education as culture. Education and culture are not yet on speaking terms in our country. Specializations should no longer be so much encouraged. There are enough of these speculative partialities to fill the infinite pigeonholes of our vast capitalist system and its multiple bureaus, the "crats," in this mechanized nation of salesmen; enough cogs are already made for capitalist wheels; enough conditioned minds turned out by universities to add up to ultimate grand frustration. Out of poor initiative, excellent conscripts, prey to violent partisanship. Not creative? As a matter of course. Fruit of the routine—the curriculum.

Then, general education by and for life in the free city should be had by *doing*—by life-experience at what tender age? The end of high-school age? Surely the teenager.

The university? No youth should be allowed to enter one until he has given unmistakable evidence not only of his interest in the principles of universality, but of some gift of perception that would make further re-search on his part among the eternal mysteries of the cosmic order seem desirable—both for him and for the society to which he belongs.

The judges?

Judges in the past have been some feature of institutional bureaucracy. *Fundamentally* educated, they would by intimate daily association know their fellows pretty well and therefore be qualified to select, elect or punish them under proper judgments. By laws made *for* people.

How senseless to speak of democracy where no faith is placed in the manhood of man and only "experts" are right. The expert? He is a man who has stopped thinking. Why? Because he "knows." Were education adequate in our democracy, the "expert" would be kept in a cell or caged, his special abnormality publicly exhibited as a warning to stop the university student, or any man in trouble.

Universities

We are beginning to realize that our universities are not worthy the cause or the name, not universal in any sense. Highly specialized trade-schools? That they are. And really mass-product, by specialists, to cover all specialties. Book-knowledge as inculcated is no feeler for life; the modern university will someday become more select and better antennae for the society it should serve as mentor. Then only will "university" mean inde-pendent findings, freely communicated to the growing citizenry, probably as much or more by television and radio. The university then should func-tion as the vision of society with the courage of an honest radical's con-viction, and as master of the deeper study of nature's *organic* laws. Mastery of nature-study in some high degree of excellence should be continual pri-mary concern in selecting the teacher even though convictions might conflict. Perhaps especially when in conflict. A true university would strive to deepen and preserve ideals of underlying principles evident as naturally superior. The university then would be the very life-line of democracy—which it should exist only to serve. This service qualifying the voter as Thomas Jefferson imagined and hoped it would.

Situated in quiet retreats appropriate to reflection and concentration upon deeper concerns of the creative mind by the student and his masters, endowed by the people themselves, these various rendezvous would be dedicated to culture and contain small groups of mature, well developed teachers tested for wisdom and light by experience. All should be able to work well together in designed storehouses of universal art, science and religion, typical not only of the culture that mankind has produced in Art, Architecture, Philosophy and the Sciences but also of the culture it is able to produce now. Books, plans, drawings and models would be available for particular intensive study by advanced students chosen by themselves to reside there because they excel, but more especially because of unmistakable *qualities of leadership.*

No longer much more of the "Professorship." Nor any perfunctory "examination." No curriculum (race-course). No standardizing of any kind. Instead we would have several "father-confessors" (it being safe by then to select them by popular vote of their fellows) to lead life in a university. Say one such leader chosen by the scientists, one by the artists, one by philosophers, one by the architects and one chosen by the poets of each state. These leaders—thus elected—would be supreme as the "university." And if one could be found, a statesman should certainly be added to this leadership; but he would be less a politician, more a philosopher or metaphysician.

The best freely chosen *by the best*—not for the average or from the "average." All would be cultured from within, educated by experience from the ground up and themselves qualified to judge men and methods. The uncommon man to lead the common man to excellence.

All the fellows of the leaders would be chosen by and for the elected father-confessors. Such fellows would be freely employed in research concerning matters of society; those they might work upon. Only those who gave proof of inner strength to grow, integrity in some one of the qualities of the departments of human life should be accepted in any university either to lead and enlighten others or to be admitted to study.

Universities should not be large but be qualified and qualifying. Why not somewhat like the old monastic institution? Only now liberalized; radical culture made free of injunction, of underground or overhead "influences"; learning protected or corrected by the people themselves from all pressures or interference. Thus might be the true *university* of democracy: universality definitely related to social progress and the arts, and well equipped by men of achievement or research. A preparation, this, for teaching or for the practice of anything spiritual—at all. For a living? No. "Vocation" no feature of any student at the university. The characteristic vocational training practiced as the higher education in this "capitalistic" educational system of ours should be renounced or cut back to special courses and practical uses, elsewhere. Trade-schools? Of course, many. It is so much harder for us to debunk and delimit these institutions of "learning" than any other of our institutions, although none need so much to go down to *roots*—radical—and to spell Nature with a capital "N."

The word "radical" means "of the *root*." Broadacre universities would be afraid *not* to go to the root with all honest radicals from the beginning of time to the day after the day after tomorrow.

Schools

The public schools?

For the schools more excellent teachers. Smaller and smaller flocks! Decentralization a natural aim in the direction of their education. Because the common school period ending in high school seems to be the most constructive period in education. The organic integration of the individual here challenges centralization.

The *big* American knowledge-factory, the *big* school—*big* anything is becoming a self-defeating institution. Our schools? How like one of the shoe factories of our industrial revolution! Our schoolhouses *look* like factories as one passes them going through American towns and villages! Unimaginative, they look more impotent spiritually than any good factory; so many prison houses for the young Western mind are the Greek abstractions still being taught there. Hand-picked but machine-embroidered our capitalist morals are not on speaking terms with Nature. Antique Roman law, or pseudo-Greek philosophy: this bookology is really by now a "craft" —the craft which the overseers of the knowledge-factory endorse as the beginning and end of wisdom. But the high school, as a school, is better than the college. And education should for a time end there; a four-year period of contact with experience now due.

Any culture center called a school in the universal city would be set in a natural park in the choicest part of the whole countryside, preferably by some flowing stream or large body of fresh water. The buildings themselves should be well designed and appointed not only as a whole, but so that "small" may be again divided into smaller units insofar as possible. Fireproof buildings fashioned of metals and glass or of other native material all universally adapted to the uses of young life growing up in sunlight to cherish the ideals of freedom, love ground, love space and enjoy light. Divided into small schools, each to contain, say, twenty-five children. Forty children would be a very large school. An outdoor game area and common hall or meeting room in common, a modeling and drafting room, a kitchen-dining-room would be characteristic of them all. Groups of three or four buildings might be arranged for a particular purpose around interior or exterior courts according to climate. Standardization would be here, again, but so used as to be given even more individual treatment. Enough ground for flower and vegetable beds would be planted and maintained by young workers alongside planted courts where they could conveniently be cultivated by the children. A callus on the palm would be a mark of honor. Rewards of merit would entirely cease or change as the character of the children working in these buildings changed. Large game and play spaces should be just beyond the courts and gardens. Each young worker would learn of the potentialities of the soil, the mysteries of mind not only by working on the soil and in it, but by educating his hand to draw or model or color what he saw of elemental nature equally well; learning to listen to music in the sounds of animal cries, wind in the trees, water flowing and falling. Learn by experience to be eye-minded because to be truly modern-minded is to be eye-minded. True *observers* are now most needed by democracy? Cultural buildings of this city-that-is-a-nation will be developed by architects themselves thus educated as children: architects free cultured workers in the arts; free themselves. Of first importance in school: *quality*— quality always the aim throughout education instead of quantity.

To learn to observe with clear-seeing eye the patterns of nature and draw them well would awaken certain faculties, but, more important, would be intimate approach to the study of all abstraction of Nature-structure: the study we call "abstraction" all being a kind of study of elemental architecture. This kind of research, going in behind the mere appearances for characteristic significant pattern, should inspire the growing design faculty of the younger generation and characterize the free city.

More perfect correlation of the faculties of the young, being actual and potential, would constitute a most important feature of all education. Eye and hand, body and mind, and what we call the soul thus becoming more sensitive to Nature and appreciative of integral rhythm. The very synthesis of being would appear.

In beautiful sunlit buildings thus organized, the everyday child of everyday Broadacres would be working in many ways. This child would be preparing food, learning how best to make it, when best to eat it, how to serve it charmingly to others; learning, meantime, not only to see clearly by learning to draw (define) what he sees but gradually taking other steps in practice to qualify himself to *build* organic structures. Of such a nature would Broadacre schools be. Youth learning to make two blades of grass grow where one, or none, grew before; seeing the spirit of that act coming alive! Spiritually and physically Broadacre boys and girls would become co-efficients of a *naturally* creative humanity. Individualists capable of intelligent coöperation with Principle, growing up thus, not mistaking personality for individuality or license for freedom except on pain of general reproof. All high school students now learning the sum of the most important of all lessons: to know the difference between the Curious and the Beautiful.

For these children practicing individual responsibility in freedom, one teacher to a group—a group, say, of from fifteen to forty pupils (or, better, apprentices) would be neither too low nor too high an average. If able to inspire such teeming young lives, teachers would be best paid of all workers in the city. Because they would have to be the best qualified as human beings. Teachers in the free city—because the city wishes to remain free—would be the most important, cherished members of society. No price for such inspiring human quality in the growing generation would be too high to be cheerfully paid by the dominant generation.

Thus in outline would be the smaller school buildings of Broadacres. Ten such organic units for every single inorganic big one that is now attempting to function in factory-like buildings on hard pavements in overgrown cities for herds of humanity; or in those experimental new schools built on the model of a circus but without any change in thought (or in crowding) except to exaggerate and continue the fictions of the conventional idea of "a happy childhood." Children would not go there to school to be trained to accept happily the subsequent blessings of employment as contented wage-slaves. The "cash-and-carry" system would be out of luck.

Source of Design—The Design Center

The Machine (capital "M") as it exists in Broadacres is settled in appropriate centers as the great means of mass experiment to determine greater ends in order to increase the flexibility and practical utility of every important human interest. For machine craft, or trade, the study of the machine would be in practical use, in either factories or homes. By way of machinery various crafts would be put into the hands of young students of organic structure. Young architects? In Broadacres, all maybe, more or less, young architects. Yes . . . and with the best means at home for experimental experience. Reluctantly I admit that to put the machine (or for that matter any modern tool of our civilization) into the hands of a body of young students at home, means the equivalent of some kind of "school." Fortunately, it would not be an "art school"; but one in which competent interpreters chosen by the foregathering apprentices themselves would actually be leaders, allied to the varied manufacturing industries they would teach to serve. With fresh impetus all kinds of appropriate patterns in these integrated style centers (we might so call them) would be inspiration to industry—for instance, the house, the motorcar, furniture, fabrics, etc., etc. —inspiration and an influence spreading over growing younger talent involved in these everyday design problems of production. Continually on every hand, in every new city of the democratic age in these circumstances, opportunities arise all along the way and some things to cherish as works of art would be produced.

Sensitive, unspoiled students (many are still to be found in our country) thus rescued from perfunctory machine education would, with varied techniques, lift the quality of many a basic commercial industry. Chosen by the industries themselves, under competent advice, there would naturally be workshops in the style centers equipped with the latest experiments in new machinery. Each style center, which should be adequately endowed for special research by interested industries, would be a quiet work place where talented young designers would grow and might remain indefinitely domiciled, spending the better part of each day working alternately in the laboratories, shops or upon the soil itself, in a way of life guided by their mentors. Students of machinery-using crafts rightly used, would be making myriads of useful things and might discover through these Broadacre experimental centers possibilities existing in the nature of many a particular craft which industries now know little or nothing about and might never discover on their own. In such fellowship research as this it would be the turn of fine art to use the machine. Modern machinery might so learn better to serve man. Broadacre City would ensure a better developed culture of a more appreciative United States, the country we have here been calling Usonia.

So let us say here that several branches of our industrial arts world might be taken for a ride to a true *beginning*. A certain number would be grouped together for the reason that they do react upon one another often to the great advantage of each just as young craftsmen should be interchangeable in the crafts to broaden the experience of each, and widen their sources of inspiration as well as of information.

Glassmaking, textiles, pottery, sheet metals-shaping, wood-working, casting in metal, printing and process reproductions: all industry in the changed circumstances of society should be willing to donate machinery, supply a competent machinist, and, to a certain extent, be eager to endow its own craft provided each of the various industries were certain of the proper management of such endowments and assured a share in results directly applicable to their own industry. Sharing benefits of design by designers especially adapted to a donor's particular field should be incentive enough for the donation.

Such experimental centers—not merely "schools"—intelligently conducted and inspired, would do much to reclaim and vitalize all American industry. Industry might soon make American lives really worthy of independence, less imitative of the culture of any foreign time or place, more aware of their value to their own time. With consumption in control of production, our own endeavor would not only help work out our own forms with style but would enable us as a nation (by example to all countries) to contribute to and be able to profit by the form and style of other nations without imitating them. Imitation should be strictly *out*, because inspiration would be largely *in*. As an architect, I see no reason why experiment centers of this character—thousands of them—each limited to say twenty workers, preferably less, should not make a good, abundant living while producing valuable articles as *examples* to help carry on the growth of organic style at home and so probably throughout the entire world. Each article so produced might have (should have) the quality of a work of art. A work that could not fail to be a genuine missionary wherever and to whom it might go.

Co-work-places such as these would naturally inspire a culture for the new aristocracy of democracy as it would be in the free city. Aristocracy? Yes, because democracy (I believe Thomas Jefferson was right) is to be the highest known form of aristocracy, wherever democracy is really understood and *grown*. Highest because not privileged but natural—innate and so secure.

The so-called style-centers would be located on land sufficient so that three or four hours a day of physical work on the soil would not only help to insure the living of the workers and of such visiting or resident artists as might be heads of the work-groups but, by correlation of facilities and faculties, be stimulating to imagination. Say, seven to nine hours each day divided between design and work in shops. Their creative imagination would be stimulated by such physical labor; gaining experience in constructions designed. Voluntary co-operation of the entire system of such a design establishment as this in day-to-day ways of life would be both subjective and objective. Subsequent educational influences upon the consumer and producer would grow by means of exemplar-television and the brochure. Well directed work would always have, as it should, real producing power. Each month a supply of usefully beautiful things would be ready for roadside markets. Good design in tapestries, table linen, cotton fabrics, clothing, table glassware, flower holders, lighting devices, window glass, mosaic, necklaces, screens, iron standards, fixtures, gates, fences,

192

fire-irons, enameled metals, etc., etc., for house or garden purposes, cast in aluminum, copper, lead, tin; practical flowerpots, architectural flower containers on a large scale, water jars, dishes, sculpture and paintings, all that is made for decoration or for use or suitable for reproduction. Designs for all media of value such as new process-reproduction of music and plays: designs in monograph for dwellings, farm buildings, industrial buildings. Or what have *you?*

Say, new solutions of such characteristic problems as the home, the gasoline station, better food packaging for immediate distribution—substitutes for the tin can—or modern distribution by cold storage. There would also be town and country dwellings, the helicopter, airplanes, trains, especially the automobile, and countless suitable objects for the complete furnishing of all these. Landscape planting of the vicinity and home environment—this would come first. Factories of many sorts would have to come out to the countryside to be attractive. Well designed features of Usonian everyday life fitted into the countryside as attractive places not only in which to work but to live in nearby. Again—according to the new scale of time-spacing, say, ten miles instead of a hundred feet.

Style center group stations would grow natural in this way and television and radio, owned by the people, broadcast cultural programs illustrating pertinent phases of government, of city life, of art work, and programs devoted to landscape study and planting or the practice of soil and timber conservation; and, as a matter of course, to *town planning* for better houses. In short, these style stations would be inspired hives of *creative* energy all bearing on the character of modern industry wherever industry touched the common life. Without hesitation or equivocation let's say that architecture would, necessarily, again become the natural backbone (and architects the broad essential leaders) of such cultural endeavor. It was ever so whenever civilization possessed a superior culture. Organic architecture is basic to all this because it is the intrinsic art of all structure whatsoever. In our own times architecture especially must be strong, as essential to life as it ever was strong and indispensable to the civilizations that have preceded ours. To keep insisting that architecture, because of its very nature, is the logical outline, the background and framework as well as the philosophic and aesthetic center-line of any true civilization—this is necessary now! Or else

193

no culture can be truly characteristic of us as a people or develop the essential inner discipline and natural strength to grow the true democratic ideal we profess.

So our Usonian style center should also become practical alcove in connection with the university. This in agrarian practices as well as in the practice of art and architecture, philosophy, archeology, and ecology. Intensive nature study would be the sound platform from which the broad abstractions of a cultural structure would spring. Wherever their location, even if not so important by our new time-scale, the center should not be too easy of access. All should have ample communication facilities, but as their work progressed their thought would be going out over the air by radio or television to the whole people while the workers themselves were sufficiently private.

No examinations, graduations, or diplomas as in schools now, if you please. But as any work-fellow showed special competence as apprentice in any special branch of art, science, or industry or evidence of unusual aptitude in any craft, after suitable experience he would be available as teacher in Broadacre schools; or for a place as designer in commercial industry. Broadacre City manufacturers would be contributors to such experimental work and would have second right to choose the more excellent apprentices. Bodies of young inspirational talent as well as associated experienced trade-machinists should be of such character that students from other schools in the many other branches of the free city would seek points of contact with their work by way of excursions made to the style centers—contact helpful to the designers and invaluable to Broadacre school students.

Such active work-units in design, were they truly dedicated and directly applied to the radical culture of indigenous style and the building of our city, would at last stimulate popular growth as light stimulates the growth of a garden. Officialdom would diminish or change its character entirely, if indeed there were need to continue its services, as we now know it.

194

PART FIVE

THE PRESENT

The Usonian

TO the Usonian! He is the American citizen. For him our pioneer days are not over! Perhaps pioneer days never should be. But the American frontier has shifted in many ways. Efficient and brave, our forebears took life in their own hands and often in the covered wagon went ever westward to clear grand new ground for more humane habitation. But they only blazed the way for another, unexpected, instrument of an efficiency that, by way of their own "rugged individualism," became the exaggeration of their own good qualities; and now unchecked this menace grows on into the curse of exaggeration of the capitalistic centralization of our big city. As consequence, inane mediocrity or vulgar profanity, we now see, has come out of our new power only to push the lives of the citizens around? With courage and strength of the grand paternal inheritance, he the pioneer was native forerunner of the type of domination we see today building its own mortal doom and naming it for a monument to progress. The milestone and gravestone—our skyscraper—in the potential cemeteries that our proudest cities are to become. The skyscraper thus used will mark the end of an epoch; put a period to the plutocratic republic of America, which the industrial revolution raised to the nth degree by the exercise of selfish inconsiderate prowess; and mark the beginning of another revolution. Machine power is running away with man and running away *from* the Western world to contaminate worlds of the "yellow man"—the East. Consequences of our own industrial revolution, not foreseen, have crossed the Pacific and

Atlantic. Perhaps our salvation will lie in what such capitalist centralization by machinery as ours is now will eventually do to the "yellow man" himself—as it has already done to the "white man." That result might be our only hope in any impending future which the nature of humankind seems to have staged for us—the coming war between dark and bright—the war between Occident and Orient—West and East. White and yellow? Yes, this impending consequence is our only hope—the atom is it?—but before that time comes the machine may have done its work for the yellow man that is already done for us. His increased numbers—say nine to one—may not be able to tip the balance in his favor.

Or else the white man must pioneer again along a frontier new to him: the frontier of Decentralization! Our democracy's only sunrise—its only true course. Such re-integrated decentralization will be met on every side by intrenched capital, scheming political interferences and the ubiquitous remittance-men; wives, widows and orphans of the insidious hidden money power and habituation of our civilization. In full force all these and more have to be placated or painfully cleared away by pioneers today working for a more honest, humane and constructive *success ideal* for man. An organic culture for the free citizen in the nation that becomes the free city depends upon the quality of the new success ideal we need. Excess "success" is now—as always—reactionary. Therefore more or less tragic. We must be transformed through the long-promised opportunity by the artifex held out by freedom or we will have lost all wars worth winning. Why, then, should American men and women, because of the profit system as we have practised it (after the British) be compelled to live any longer according to the exaggeration of the baser qualities of our nature? Why not work now more patiently for a simple, natural ideal made right end to and right side up for man to live by? Good enough to live by and according to the light of his natural better self? Doing so, our nation will not only survive but will enable all the rest of the world to thrive and, at the same time, make innate the only impregnable "defense" our nation has or any nation may have.

The New Pioneer

So, pioneering on this *new frontier* should not again come down to merely scraping off the too full bushel while ignoring the now legalized industrial impositions that continually overfill it again. The tinker, the soldier, the politician, the professor—all the best imitators and salesmen of vicarious power—is this the best power of which we as a people seem capable? Well, if it is infallibly to be on that basis, we are the tail end of a civilization! The *end*, not the middle, not even the beginning of a great one.

Statesmanship we now require! As a scientific art, "the art of human happiness," we of these United States have lost it to that promise-merchant —the politician! Mediocrity has risen to high places by way of the profit taker's desires? No, his necessities.

A good statesman would be naturally a scientist, an architect of human happiness. He would be pilot, too, of an organic social order. What politician today, then, can we call a statesman? Reforms the politicians propose (sometimes) are but the political propaganda of our promiscuous governing powers, themselves governed by their own bureaucracy; usually little more than petty shifts to and fro in the complex rules intended to regulate and standardize money getting by using old laws on the statute books and repudiating the welfare of the citizen; old makeshifts that have been tried so many times and in so many ways and places that our new civilization is now likely to be defeated, destroyed by suicidal artificiality such as ours has become by conformity.

Sensible interpretation, either economic or spiritual, of our changed circumstances on the new frontier has not yet been contrived and so has not been fairly tried. A great people with a great ideal, we have been stultified if not betrayed by appeal to the votes of the mass ignoramus. Mostly betrayed by ourselves, of course, so ruthlessly invading other countries simply or largely because we have lost the true meaning of our own! However we here admit we are scared enough to pretend to be eager to "liberate" other nations! We must face it! We are unable to recognize or intelligently meet the drastic changes now due our own machine age growth of money power as a substitute for ideas. Spiritually we, in our own great nation, are still living in a neglected backyard from coast to coast. Where beauty of environment is concerned we do not understand its value; nor do we understand the devastating, or liberating, values of important organic changes taking place—to our own immense advantage. If we could but learn to practice, much less defend, what we call—without real comprehension—Democracy! Instead we now "defend" only what we consider our "interests." So we go from war to war—sciences used only to run away in order to go to war again some other day? The same old new way now by science improved? Whereas the only impregnable human defense we have on earth is faith in ourselves and in our own kind. Our own unafraid performance here at home will make us or break us.

Nature

Hitherto any capital mind among us has seriously questioned the right-mindedness and good instincts of other humankind. When and wherever humanity itself, *disciplined from within by an ideal,* is free, this is not so. In what, then, does equitable freedom consist in our already overgrown but so far underdone society? Let us truly and freely discuss our malady, sincerely seek the probable remedy, and discover the underlying basis of all growth and decay. Then we will find the basis we know to be organic. Only in that search may we discuss our order of freedom as a natural order or discuss the natural order of economics and the causes of war and debt intelligently, and as frankly as we discuss biology, for instance. Then, I believe, the fundamental democracy which we profess would come right side up for us—and so soon. Facing ourselves, as we must, and asking ourselves the right questions would truly add up the forces of our machine and money power. We, ourselves, of the New World, must go to work first to gain our own integrity: then, our feet well under us on firm ground, work *with* the world for peace, never *upon* it by war. We all know this. Why are we unable to practice it or even preach it by our own acts?

Let us ask ourselves these necessary questions: In what lies the significance of human life in which machine power has grown to be the destructive factor that it now is in the hands of money power? When clearly distinguished from life in various other forms of the social contract, in what (really) does human honor or even true machine efficiency consist at this time? Where and as we now live, can we use the usurious, vicarious powers of the machine here at home and continue to grow as happy human beings by forcing overproduction on the world at our own expense?

What now, then, is good sense? Incidentally, how would a *natural* economic order touch us here at home as the orthodox money matter now stands? Organic law teaches that we can hammer heated iron but not a stick of dynamite. Just so we need more serious study of *organic* law everywhere because it has been so completely ignored by avaricious money and land power. We have too much of the blinding externalities as well as the manifest disadvantages of ancient Roman law we have adopted by way of Oxford and Cambridge as paternal influences.

Are we to face ourselves and ask these vital questions and find answers aright? Are we patiently to investigate the present uneconomic basis of our life, such as it is, and learn *why* it has to go to war because it has no organic foundations and therefore is forever *unsafe?* Why has this matter, fundamental to us all, had so little study all down the line? Must we go on from war to war? Why not now reinterpret the significant facts of our own history as assembled and interpreted by honest radicals all too familiar with the nature of the root as well as the character of our finance? We must learn why our orthodox money system is a wholly inorganic superstructure. No *foundation* at all is there! Only an expedient assumption. Patiently we must learn why our life is now so inorganic, so wasteful and dangerous. Just as we must learn why the classic architecture we have adapted, or adopted, is four-fifths false, expedient inartistic waste of our natural opportunity; and try to realize why anything inorganic may have sporadic increase but *can never produce or reproduce itself as Life*. We must know why, wherein and in whatever of our circumstances, the complete correlation essential to *true growth* is lacking and that nothing can really grow from within—either for us, in us or by us—until our economic as well as spiritual foundations are *by nature* secure.

Only *entity* lives, only entity can reproduce! That is why capitalist centralization in cities is no longer the expansion of humane opportunity but fatal contradiction of structure and so a stricture. This innate contradiction is growing. It is a strong arm, unnatural, having no interior expanding principle of its own; no real integrity from within is possible to its character. Manifold "efficiencies" of our so-called money "system" is too urban, too involved on the surface with artificialities to function for democratic manhood's own good! Our money system is involution, incapable of true evolution. It can only add, subtract, multiply and divide—especially divide.

To such false strictures human life in these United States is now too narrowly committed. Life in our republic attempting democracy cannot be committed to centralism (such as our money system also represents) except to stultify and degenerate its manpower. If we persist, we too must die as such false but expedient commitments have ever died. History holds the proof. Why not read the proof?

As our present uneconomic systems are inorganic, no matter how gigantic and all pervasive, so the social system of our life must be even more so— and our philosophy, our art, our religion remain more or less parasitic! Shall our "foreign policies" be blind and our fate eventually tragic. Why do our domestic politics continue so confused or blind and futile? American statesmanship in the light of any honest interpretation of the spirit of democracy is now misleading or inadequate. Our status quo by statesmanship *always* lies hidden from us. Is it because it is always some form of conscription?

For the same or a similar reason our great fortunes are with us, largely false, too unproductive unless by unfair taxation.

So have we drifted so far away from the valiant original intent of the democratic ideal of our great republic! So many ignoble forms of hidden selfishness, inane exaggerations of self, mistaken for selfhood. And by the very forces we have elevated for hire, in some form—some form of rent— we are now continually drawn downward by exaggerated forms of urbanism. Thoughtless uses of the vicarious power we agree to call Money by our credulous faith in the "substitute." Money power itself is only another vicarious power—and vanishes. Sources of money seem more important to us than the family and home, than the sources of life itself. What fate for such power as our industrialism becomes? The portals will open and the cartels get you, Mr. Vicarious-Power-Man. And soon!

To Have and to Hold

One of the main perversions of the principles of our democracy is to allow land to hold improvements made on it by the man who lives upon and improves and loves the land. What folly to have turned over his credit, existing only by way of the people of a great nation, to middlemen exalted officially to exercise a broker's takings: the broker himself being the banker's banking system. What tragic finality for our industrial revolution to have turned the citizen himself over to the machine as the slave of production—himself made only another kind of machine—all this done in order to concentrate and maintain more money power. Centralization that proves of fictitious value except as the war master becomes incontinent waster of human quality.

So it is by means of our borrowed culture and the specious middleman we have bred in all departments of our activity that we now reach a dubious debt era—the era of the front-runner and the useful substitute. Have we reached this degradation wherein all is more or less a kind of makeshift? Our very best is no more, at present at least, than adventitious? True? Then we ourselves can likely become no more than just that; and our life and our architecture have no organic (normal) foundation at all. And if so fundamentally wrong there at the root, how can American life ever genuinely become free? The valiant special man (non-common) among us—he alone is free. But even so he is free at his own peril; enemy, and therefore the dislike of the common man pursues him to some bitter end for both.

As things have been with us (now still more so) honest individual freedom, non-conformity, is growing to be a desperate, dangerous adventure for any loyal citizen. I have described true discipline as developed from within, as the expression of the soul instead of something applied by force in some form. As things are, the freedom won by such discipline will only be something on the way to the country poorhouse. Or to jail. We will come to this day of reckoning?

Nevertheless, out of observation of principles of organic architecture at work—with law-abiding respect for the law of natural change in this most successful of all nations—comes this ideal of a true capitalist city designed

202

actually to harness and utilize the terrific forces that built us into the present whirling vortex from the top down.

Can we be a free people and be tolerant of mere *re*form when true form is what we should seek? No form true to our own nature will be made by mere alteration upon any old systems or architecture or old laws we have in desperation cherished. True forms, especially of independence in our modern lives, can only grow up from within the nature of our common life as we live it with our feet on our own soil however high our head in the clouds. Evolution? Perhaps revolution is a necessary feature. I do not know. As Nature herself grows forms so human nature—*her own higher nature*—must always grow buildings, civilizations, on good ground; West and East at last so reconciled as to work independently together. The light of the West is the light of the diamond, iridescent like the stars. The light of the East glowing incandescent like that of colored gems burning with the lovely light of Earth in the palm of the hand. Why then hate and war with each other? All go to make a proper diadem for civilization—a Culture. And it will take all kinds to make a free world.

So I do venture to believe we as a nation have carried abroad enough good tidings to compensate for our sorrow over wrongly concentrated machine power. This mechanized era may go on with renewed faith, beneath all suffering, go to the root—and radically design the structure of a characteristic organic culture. To succeed in this uncommon endeavor we must commence work square with a fresh perception of *nature's organic laws* as they are now manifest—and actually change wherever or in whatever degree we are able to find and fit our course to them. In architecture we call this recognition of principle "organic" and cultivate "continuity" as a science. It is also the art of equilibrium in all human opportunity. To learn to perceive it is to learn the inevitable purpose of our own Life.

To have and to hold! Yes—well enough when having and holding square *with* nature; but disastrous, if not fatal, unless *giving* and *taking* according to nature! What I write here is directly in line with normal continuity in the law of organic change. As an architect I have observed these laws at work not only in and upon materials of building construction but also upon men and women throughout the vast undeveloped reaches of our already over-exploited country. Yes—in the light of this organic ideal—a vast beautiful region from coast to coast and border to border, undeveloped and sadly in need of synthesis.

Time then, for these importunate powers we have been describing to be recognized by politics and education as mere scaffolding of the civilization we—the core of the modern free world—still fervently desire, however we may have betrayed it. Unfortunately, we have now gone so far afield as to mistake the scaffolding for our civilization. Such vital forces as we do have have won so little intelligent recognition. Our machine age culture (the elevation of the ground-plan of our plight) can now afford recognition of no force not really creative! No present commitment we have made to brute force by bomb or mentality can reproduce from seed because the true greatness of a people like ours does not lie in centralized wealth and science promoted and distinguished from profound Art, Architecture and Religion. These three are the soul of a culture. From the union of these with Science comes the freedom of a people.

But I confess that adventitious money increment—a power derived from exaggerated centralization used, as we are now using it, as incentive to desperate human effort—has not been utterly wasted. The techniques released by our machine age have been more rapidly developed than would have been the case otherwise, and that speed is part of our trouble. It may mean more imminent disaster at the point the atom bomb has reached where mechanical forces are running away with man. But such material gains as these might be consciously utilized in the objective *structure* of the new city in our new social state as in our economics and our morals, and—especially now—in our aesthetics also. But can the questionable materialistic "advantages" which centralization has brought to the manhood of our country be justified by the ghastly cost of these "efficiencies" in business, in government, in society, in sportdom no less?

Has not the time come to revaluate our course? Or else we will leave on record no true advance in beneficent civilization. We will have the shortest life of any civilization on record.

Any attempted slavery to material life employed in the name of democ-

204

racy is folly. The machine and democracy, standing bound together as they are, are fast growing wide apart, only to destroy each other eventually. But by way of each other, they are capable of new vital form and expression in modern art, even in religion as already we have seen in science. But until science is qualified by art and religion truly free and reconciled to both, in co-operation and inspiration vital to new art forms to enrich the spirit, human misery will only deepen.

Again the setting sun all Europe mistook for dawn?

Latter-day Civilization

Well . . . inwardly I believe that we must recognize openly and use the good in these strange new forms now thrusting at our cities against base imitations (conscious or unconscious) of dead forms now trying so hard and by dishonest means to hide the lack of any significance.

Education is unable to recognize (or unwilling to face) the fact that in these potent changes by mechanical agencies, conscientiously enumerated here, we must turn about to subdivide growing aggregates of machine power, abolish invisible despotisms, and advocate *radical* revision of the growing governing agencies—our bureaucracy. Revisions are necessary now to release and encourage the spirit of human initiative; help broaden, officially and socially, the *voluntary* basis of native manpower; develop and fortify the conscience of the citizen, defend it as inviolate to democracy.

Good education would consist in patiently building up the manly attributes of character that are the basis of true individuality but which we are allowing this machine age to destroy. Education must no longer ignore the fact that democracy proclaims the sovereignty of the individuality? Must our education (like government) continue static because it is organized deeply to distrust Man? And is science able to give us no faith in man as mankind but only tend to take it away?

Democracy in Overalls

The dream of the free city is to establish democracy on a firmer basis. . . . Is it a dream? A vision certainly. Ideas always precede and configure the facts. But I am here writing no more than the too specific outline of a practical ideal perceiving Change as already upon us. Old phases as well as phrases must come to an end. Graphic and plastic arts and fine art come in at this point to aid in showing just what the universal city and its buildings might be. The different buildings here described have already been given either graphic (the drawing) or three-dimensional (the model) form. To begin, I believe that a general outline of any ideal is better than specific plan or model of its particular features. An ideal once clearly fixed in mind —and the plan will come naturally enough. Fresh undertakings then appear and proceed from generals to particulars with the necessary techniques peculiar to each. True ideas must develop their own technique afresh: The higher the ideal at first the more important and difficult the technique.

To the impatient, critical reader and all architectural eclectics who have come along thus far, these all too broad outlines of the coming free city may seem only one more "Utopia" to join so many harmless dreams that come and go like glowing fireflies in July meadows. But I am not trying to prove a case. My interest lies in sincerely appraising, in our own behalf, elemental changes I see existing or surely coming. There is plenty of evidence now at hand to substantiate all the changes I outline. At least here you have an earnest architect's conscientious study of organic structure ahead based upon manifest circumstances and the experience of a lifetime trying to get organic architecture to come alive as the true-form-of-building for American Democracy. An architect's struggle (so it is) in these United States lies in trying to get any profound study of any sort in the Arts into good form. I am seeing and saying that organic architecture is the only true architecture for our democracy. Democracy will some day realize that life is itself architecture organic, or else both architecture and mankind will become in vain together.

As a people no doubt we are busy sacrificing the greater usefulness and the only happiness we can ever know in our own name to put our all into the cheaper, lesser "efficiencies," expedient as I see them. It is useless to go

206

on further working for the senseless mechanisms of mere machinery for the landlord, the machine lord and his lady (as they stand) hoping for any sound general profit for the great future culture of this nation—and for the culture of this world. Noble life demands a noble architecture for noble uses of noble men. Lack of culture means what it has always meant: ignoble civilization and therefore imminent downfall.

The true center (the only centralization allowable) in Usonian democracy, is the individual in his true Usonian family home. In that we have the nuclear building we will learn how to build. Integration is vitally necessary to that normal home. Natural differentiation just as necessary. Given intelligent, free, individual choice the home should especially cherish such free choice—eventually based upon a greater range of possible freedom, range for such individual choice in the specific daily cultivation of principles in Architecture as well as in the daily uses we make of Science and Art. In Religion? No less!

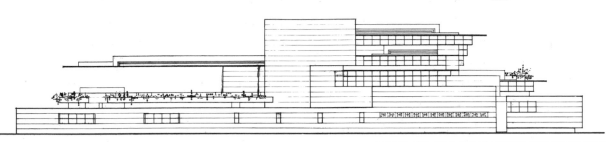

HOUSE ON THE MESA, NORTHEAST ELEVATION

Luxury (it, *too*, is primarily a matter of individual quality) would enter the democratic social sense as gratification of more and more developed humane *sensibility*, beauty the concern. Exuberance is beauty but not excess. Yes. Liberty is not license, exaggeration is not exuberance. Every true home should be actually bound to grow from within to dignity and spiritual significance: *grow* by the right concept and practice of building into a pervasive social circumstance: *grow* out of one's own good ground and better self into everybody's light, not in everybody's nor anybody's way. Every man's home his "castle!" No, every man's home his sphere in space—his appropriate place to live in spaciousness. On his own sunlit sward or in wood or strand enhancing all other homes. No less but more than ever this manly home a refuge for the expanding spirit of man the individual. This home is for the citizen of Usonian democracy, our teenager. In *his own home* thus the Broadacre citizen would be not only impregnable. He would be inviolate. This nation indestructible! He would be true exponent of a man's true relationship to his fellow-men because he *is* his fellow-man. He *is* his country. So he would naturally inculcate high ideals in others by practicing them himself. He would insist upon opportunity for others to do no less. External compulsions, personal or official, were never more than weakness continually breeding weaknesses or weaklings. Usonian home-makers of Broadacres would first learn to know all this so well that the citizen would practice this knowledge instinctively in his every public act, not only to the benefit of others who come in contact with him but to gratify something deep in his very nature.

The Awakened Citizen

Improvements. Well, "improvements" in the sense of this sense of self are not only on but *of* the ground. Actually they belong to those who make the improvements and learn to use them as features of their own life; use

HOUSE ON THE MESA — THE LUXURY HOUSE

HOUSE ON THE MESA, LIVING ROOM

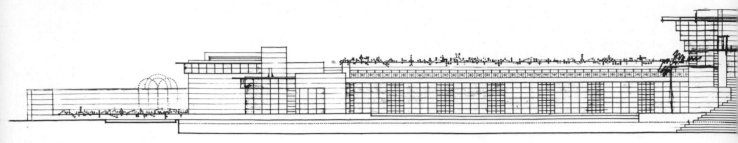

SOUTH — EAST ELEVATION

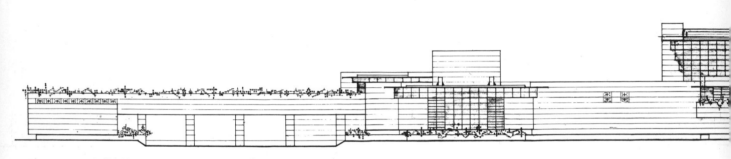

NORTH — WEST ELEVATION

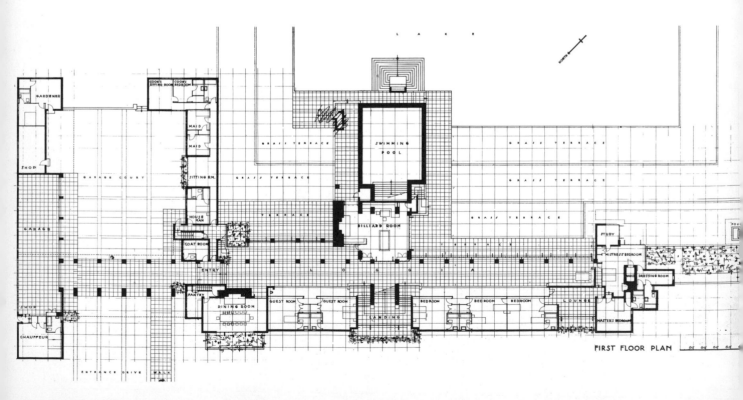

FIRST FLOOR PLAN

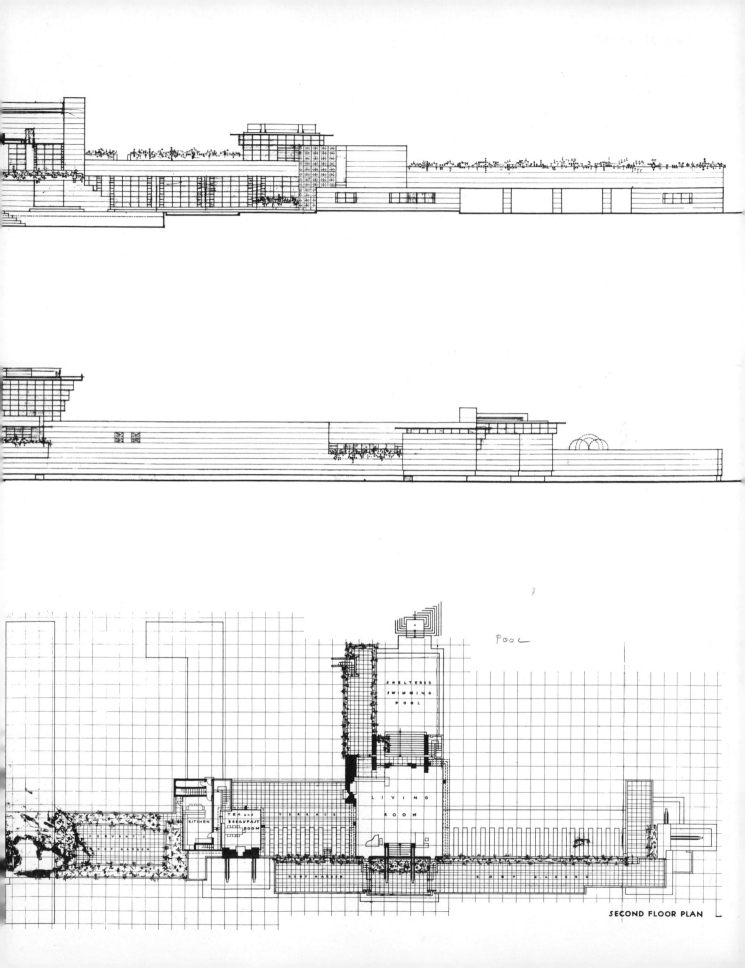

POOL

SHELTERED
SWIMMING
POOL

LIVING

ROOM

KITCHEN

TEA and
BREAKFAST
ROOM

TERRACE

SERVANT'S
ROOF GARDEN

ROOF GARDEN

ROOF GARDEN

SECOND FLOOR PLAN

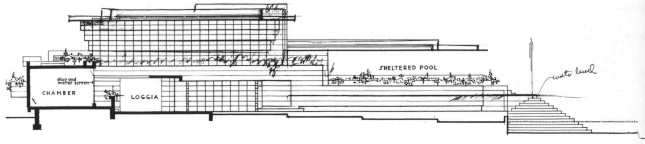

SECTION THRU BED ROOM AND S.-W. ELEVATION

them well in relation to other lives. It would make sound economic sense for the homeowner to surround himself with all such ideal expressions as might seem square with his ideal. He could no longer be compelled to pay unjust penalties for so doing. Advantages flow naturally in upon the enlightened and enlightening democratic unit in this new humane stronghold. Well aware of these, the significance of much that he knew but never realized comes clear. In worldly situations, radical changes necessarily due to fundamental realizations of freedom would render obsolete most of his old educational paraphernalia: destroy nearly all the so-called "traditions" once cherished by his teachers. He *knew* this, but now he *realizes* it. Then to what may he hold fast as he finds himself able to go forward to new life in this new way on his own ground? Power is now to become his own responsibility—power never dreamed of until he thus began to live as a free man. Power now is perpetually renewed from within himself, power appropriate to his new circumstances.

Production with a capital *P* has previously battened and fattened upon the homemaker. At exorbitant rent he has painfully acquired utilitarian conveniences by debt and such modern sanitation as the homemaker may have in this present day of the runaway industrial revolution. But all these and more may now be made from the bottom up and from inside out into one single unit *for him*. Convenience, ten to one in point of economy and true beauty (they are one now) may be his and do for him what he could not ask of "conveniences" heretofore: Electrification, sanitation, gadgetry of the kitchen complete, all utilities lacking individuality, to be delivered to him as is his car, in prefabricated units. Composing the characteristic Usonian abode, great variety of individual choices exists. Choice would naturally *increase* as the new materials—glass, steel, sheet metal, and the new plastics—let his life expand, *understood*. Vision comes into grounds surrounding and he places appropriate gardens around him. Vistas of the landscape become part of his house and life just as his house becomes integral part of neighborhood landscape. The machine properly disciplined by good design brings tangible, fruitful benefits to the homemaker by space interior and exterior—the new time-space concept, as described earlier. What that may mean to his spirit as well as his comfort lies easily within his reach. Luxury for him will consist in his new sense of a harmony—space free is his. However simple this house, it will be well designed and planned *with him for him*: good materials in good design, well executed. To be himself, the Broadacres homemaker will exercise his new sense in the ground plan of the place he is to live in, as well as the scheme of things around him, the spirit that made it free will maintain it so. The reward and refuge of such life as this would be in the free city would consist largely in fresh opportunity to have and to hold his own shelter secure by his own effort in his own atmosphere, free to go, stay or come. And whenever, however, he pleases to go, there is always something nearby worth seeing—a pleasure to go to.

Every man's new standard of space-measurement (we have said it is the man seated in his car) affects him everywhere he goes, and he can go anywhere. But, most of all, the new sense of space affects him where and how he may live. New breadths, increased depths, not only in the simple reaches of the new building he proudly calls home but into the very makeup of his faith in freedom. A feature of his philosophy realized. Thus inner sense of security defends him against imposition leading eventually to "repossession." And it will be just as hard to scare this Usonian out of his sense or his home as to scare him out of himself. The Usonian citizen will find new faith in himself, on his own acreage no longer a man to be afraid or to be afraid of. He will not "huddle." Nor will he run with the pack! Ask him. His faith is in—what?

Now because the American citizen will learn how expanded light, spacious openness and firm cleanliness of significant line in oneness of the whole may be his own, and how all may add to his stature as a man among men, he will not be stampeded. More chary than ever of grandomania, either at home or abroad: to this richly animated, awakened citizen's imagination quiet repose appeals most because beauty is concerned with him and he with beauty. With a sense of rhythmic quality in the appropriateness of plane to quiet length of line, he is able to trace the flowing simplicity of melodious contours of structure as he sees them in what he does to the land itself. Learns from it. The grace of native flowers in garden or meadow or by the roadside—he truly sees—the trees in teeming life of the wood or landscape. Naturally all will be a refreshing feeling of intimacy with Nature; grateful for space to be lived in; the new spaciousness understood, deeply enjoyed. In his new life the truth is he himself "belongs!" Even as hill-slopes, or the beautiful ravines and forests themselves belong and as bees and trees and flowers in them belong so *he* belongs. While at home, the citizen is pleased and pleasing lord of space. He has integrity. Spacious interior freedom becomes him and is the *new reality*. Romantic: he is both introvert and extrovert. No longer is his faith placed in arbitrary hangovers of Roman law because he goes deeper to the organic law beneath. There in Nature is where his new faith in himself is founded and can be defended.

Both physical and spiritual significance his, oneness of life lies in this new more natural sense of himself. The citizen is bound to see and find tremendous spiritual consequences come alive in him. For all of life, love, and the pursuit of happiness is no longer a phrase. It is the architecture of his soul.

Why, then, should citizenry ever be small, dishonest or mean? Why should the citizen deny to others what he has learned to value so highly within himself? Out of independence such as his a new idea of man emerges. He co-operates because it is for him to say either "Yes" or "No" and say so *as his own conscience dictates*!

214

Romance

This interior sense of space in spaciousness is romantic and growing throughout the world. Well understood, it is the true machine age triumph, a true luxury. And as this sense of space in spaciousness becomes innate to mankind, I believe the American citizen will develop a more concrete freedom than a Greek or a Roman ever knew or even the Goth felt in the Middle Ages. Or any freedom to which West or East has subscribed or aspired. Perhaps greater in range of freedom interior, to go with freedom exterior, than man ever believed could be unless, perhaps, some adventurer like the ancient Arab or American Indian, some romantic like Francois Villon, or people of the earth-loving East sensed, "once upon a time." In sweep, simplicity (especially *in quality*), architecture never surpassed in significance and beauty what may be this awakened citizen's architecture—that of the free City that is a Nation. Again—that new city is nowhere unless everywhere.

Space comes alive, to be enjoyed and lived in, characteristic of this age of the machine. This is our growth, spiritual integration with everyday life. Simple because it is universal conservation of life, happiness is inevitable consequence.

Architecture

Such practice of life lies in the province of organic architecture: architecture sure to react upon every practical homemaker's sense of himself. Modern man cannot fail to grow in health of mind as he becomes aware of himself as free. He *is* freedom! Freedom at home makes all men doubly democratic in spirit: Any man now demands the freedom for other men and their nations that he asks for himself because only so may he demand freedom as his "inalienable" *right*? It will not now be too difficult for the Broadacre citizen to see "his" right as no more than "their" right. When the meaning of the word "organic" dawns within the mind of the man, he will demand integrity and significance in everything he has to live with or that he does to others. His awakened eye will see boldly and he will not hesitate to search habitual forms everywhere, rejecting forms he once took for granted when he was only educated not cultured. He now challenges all form. The Usonian of Broadacres will have truth of form or he will have none! This goes out from him to his familiars and to establish better economic and social relations with other nations. It goes out from him to characterize American life—no curse put upon the world by insane exhortations of business to increase private "production" for greater public waste.

The citizen of Broadacres would see political science too as something organic—"the science of human happiness." And see economics that way too. He would reject state department banking and trading as likely to be vicious. Broadacres citizens would also regard philosophy as organic. The simplicities of Laotze and those of Jesus would dawn afresh. To practice them he would learn to find them concrete, effective *forces* that really work. At last the citizen would see that the inner forces at work in his life are organic and therefore prophetic.

Discipline

So *interior discipline of an Ideal* thus set up in the citizen will go to work. Undreamed of potentialities show in the work of the workman as he becomes responsible to *himself* for himself. He is the only *safe* man because he is the man now disciplined not by government (the police) but from within by himself! Herein lies the great social potential worthy of the greatest of human works of art and science. Democracy itself.

So free men will soon walk abroad in modern times, nobler men among nobler-minded manhood—more than ever potent in making a fairer-minded world. A better sense of proportion now to go with his sense of humor and his true sense of himself.

As world citizen the Usonian's power no longer lies in peddling or meddling or borrowing or lending or becoming stupidly mischievous with money "abroad." Power no longer in the control of vicarious officialism at public expense. Individual aspiration would never consist in or subsist on imitating anything. First of all—for all—quality. Only because of well-founded confidence in his own strength will man be eager to *share* in the

216

work of the world. The world will be invigorated by his happiness because it will have the vitality of good sense. His actual practice of the democracy we preach will be no less inspiring. Were the world to see this citizen, results would become ideal for all the world. Exemplar in his own life in his own home, feet on his own ground! See a man free, alive.

"Where There Is No Vision the People Perish"

Here, then, a vision? I give you the ideal *practical* democrat: he the Usonian citizen of the great free city of this book. No longer impotent robot: he the potent citizen of the new natural city that is taking place among us already. Then comes a nation as example to free the whole world, to prove that freedom is not several but ever one and indivisible! Practical become integral.

The Wage Slave

Tillers of the fields, owing to universal electrification and mobility, today may enjoy anything the big city offered the wage-slave of yesterday as reward. White-collarites and industrialists, parasites immured, restless, longing to go from here to there where establishment insures full measure of occupation at work they like. Widening margins of leisure everywhere the machine now insures: a margin that does not mean more or less unemployment for anyone but more time to spend as the independent workman may like to spend time. The workman citizen of our nation must see his native birthright as green: the green of the ground. Once there free on his own, by his own character, skill and voluntary labor he is bound to succeed in "the pursuit of happiness." No other secure basis for happiness is as intelligent as good *use* of good ground. Then, why not go there and learn how—or learn how and go there?

Industrial occupations may then grow to mean to him so much more that no official guaranty of urban "employment" is good enough for him. His own initiative and consciousness of manhood *protected*, here at home!

There is no longer reason for a man of good conscience to doubt that all that he is or may become should not work in full harmony *with* other men according to nature and each man be secure in the nature of himself. Therefore all mankind secure. His own nature may be so attuned to the nature of the cosmos that he in himself would be a new, more vital, kind of success. Only through such interior organic process is he (or are we) going to be able to build the city of democracy.

Do you question this Fundamental direction for American citizens of the future? Then first learn the meaning of these words.

"Organic."

"Decentralization."

"Integration."

"Democracy."

Words never properly identified by the American citizen because never properly interpreted to him in action. Then how could the words be applied by him or to his work or his life in this or any culture, ancient or modern? They were misunderstood or misapplied terms by civilization after civilization—civilizations now dead.

The significance of these words (watchwords) may now belong to the awakened American citizen. Qualifications at last for his "vote." An understanding opens to the significance of the law of change—what is insignificant in life fades, falls away as the inner meaning of the words comes clear. Inevitably he will come face to face with *this* new reality in the words of Laotze: *"The reality of the building does not consist in the four walls and roof but in the space within to be lived in."* The significance of this lies where his life is now concerned—with these words.

Former practices of the vicarious power that once meant fortune will leave the twentieth century industrialist all but useless. He was a worker immured in government, in housing or some form of conscription. A conscript to be cast aside. But in the free city homemaking for manhood can mean spiritual stagnation no more nor strangulation of his finer sensitivities. Work, and his home, must be the honor of his own better self. "Home" only then having all the meaning and privileges it must have in genuine Democracy. New spirit forces are now going to work upon our vast material resources in this new direction—material resources worked upon by what-

218

ever spiritual force the free man has left to him. All this force opens to the citizen if he should so decide. No man need be a kept or "Yes" man; if he goes intelligently to his birthright in nature he is now independently a "No" man, if he so chooses. Here now we have the broad base of capital where it belongs—on the ground—the base of the pyramid no longer up in the air.

Only the democratic citizen liberated can put to work forces that make the machine no longer a destructive imposition upon human life, elevating instead of exhausting man's innate spiritual power. Spiritual force in a way of life wherein man feels, thinks, and learns to live anew as a *natural aristocrat*. The ideal Usonian aristocrat, the American citizen could, if he would, use the word "aristocracy" honestly in describing the great new city. A great integrity.

Now here at last, we have capitalism for genuine Democracy. The capitalist himself his own impregnable defense!

Night Is but a Shadow Cast by the Sun

Looking back over this book I see it was not written to *please* anyone, not even myself. The same urge impelling me to build has impelled me to write. The book began, 1932, as *The Disappearing City*. 1945, it was expanded into *When Democracy Builds*. Now here entirely rewritten as *The Living City*.

This matter (a direct continuous study beginning 1921) was first presented as "The City" in a lecture at Princeton University. Subsequently that lecture was published with five others by the Princeton University Press. While in Arizona, pushed there by the national breakdown of 1929, the Broadacre City model—12 feet by 12 feet—was made by the Taliesin Fellowship. It was first exhibited at the Industrial Arts Exposition, Radio City, New York, April 15, 1935. This modeling is now a feature of Taliesin.

Does "The Art and Craft of the Machine," the paper first read at Hull House, 1903 (since translated into seven languages), seem to suffer contradiction here?

No. I then dreaded the machine *unless well in the hand of the creative artist*. Saying so then, I say so now. I knew then that this power we call the Machine was, otherwise, socially malevolent. The creative artist (culture his consideration), I believed, would be in the place where he belongs in a civilization ready to accept the machine but only as a new tool: a new facility capable of improving or destroying man on earth. Well . . . he is not there where he belongs. "The machine" is cutting him off on the ground! He must begin at the beginning again at the root—a radical.

But today the Machine is running away. I find it hard to believe that the machine would go into the creative artist's hand even were that magic hand in true place. It has been too far exploited by industrialism and science at expense to art and true religion.

Machine facilities have increased inordinate quantity production beyond consumption until total mechanization is trying to control distribution and the market. By total industrialism war, more war is always in sight, paid for in advance—all but the bloodshed. The machine is now become more the engine of destruction, and propaganda for increasing our national insecurity by wage-slavery is everywhere in the social fabric of the news. Higher human faculties, which the machine should serve to release in our Democracy, are officially and academically emasculated, the humane interest fast disappearing. That is why the belated rewriting of this—seeming to me now —more timely, more important than ever book, original advocate of organic architecture; again to take the stand for the consumer (the people) as against the ubiquitous, thoughtless producer for profit. The "consumer" now must take what "production" decides to make. Whatever production decides to make, for profit, is all the consumer can get in any line. This antithesis of the democratic process is a menace, a drift toward deadly conformity. For the sake of conformity, we the people get quantity defying quality.

Owing largely to facility beyond our means, since time immemorial no blacker time for Principle has existed than our own "present." Of course, our "present" is no exception to all the "present" there ever was in time, as history is written.

If the advertising we see spread by the "big-production boys" is indicative of our commercial activity, no lasting benefit of our bomb-throwing extravaganzas on foreign soil will ever get over to us as we live here. Must we of this nation—free—wait for the vitality and depth of a right-minded inevitable free city? The pattern is not to come from "over there." We, if square with the ideal of Democracy, must make a new city. Must we wait for our big-production boys to "cash in" and go to spend their hard-gained profits in heaven or hell, maybe? Of course, *à la mode*—but what mode?

Plainer to me every day that not only our professional streamliners—experts (hired for the back-rooms of our big-production boys)—see nothing yet of the citizen's first needs first. The big boys have yet seen nothing at all of *interior* nature on their own.

Production is trying too hard to manufacture the same old things, in a reversion of the same old ignorance of good design that built creatures of the hand, and to manufacture them by *negation of that hand*. Now in a dead house for dead men. And trying, too, to make themselves believe it is a brand new way! How can anyone with half a mind tolerate eventual negation such as this not only of the man who makes the house but of any man who gets the house to live in? And by house I mean also the city and the nation. Negation of Democracy itself is—and therefore—inevitable: a mere matter of time. Education seems to know little or worse. The old steel post and girder framing of the nineteenth century bridge engineer is still a rigid concept to the "expert" in twentieth century architecture. Not one but builds from outside inward instead of from inside outward. Yet the talk is "modern."

Probably our many big city survivals (yes, feudal—plus gadgetry) will escape destruction from inside if not overhead only to find their originals (European cities devastated by us) replanned and built more nearly as a modern city should be than ours. We have had no benefit from the devastating bomb ourselves except to make the bomb, market it and drop it ourselves over "on the other side." So we are likely, as things are, to find ourselves far outmoded by any standard of comparison when the smoke of destruction clears away in the light of reconstruction and V for Victory may look more like V for Vanquished.

Finally, then, this long discourse, hard to write or read, is a sincere attempt to take apart and show (from the inside) the radical simplicities of fate to which our own machine skills have now laid us wide open and try to show how radical eliminations are now essential to our spiritual health, and to the culture, if not the countenance, of democratic civilization

221

itself. These are all changes valid by now if we are to have indigenous culture at all and are not to remain a bastardized civilization with no culture of our own, going all the way down the backstairs of time to the usual untimely end civilizations have hitherto met.

Wholesome destruction may eventually *compel* an open change for improvement that our young architects must accept as a challenge. They can be equal (I think so) to the tremendous task only by seizing upon urban obsolescence to destroy these rubbish-heaps that are with us here at home. Do this by learning how to help the inevitable natural city to go on building itself: the right kind of buildings, built the right way in the right place for the right people—this, and the right kind of city will grow for us. But I see a studied avoidance of such interference by mediocre professional meddlers as a feature of the new "planning" we do not need.

"The Living City" then is nothing less than inspiration, or better, than restraint upon the effects of ill planning by the trustees whose responsibility it is—our young architects.

I hope this architect's book is at least an exhortation for them, a warning for the farmer, a caution and encouragement for the small manufacturer and for national colleges of architecture and agriculture, or such cultural nurseries in this nation as the machine age has raised or razed or carelessly left standing. We cannot achieve our democratic destiny by mere industrialism, however great. We are by nature gifted as a vast agronomy. In the humane proportion of those two—industrialism and agronomy—we will produce the culture that belongs to Democracy organic. And in the word "organic" lies the meaning of this discourse. So this book is all the more for that great invisible but potent "in-between"—that new *reality* we call, here, his majesty the American citizen.

Democracy! Can we in these United States of America make it work? Or will we in honesty change the name of the politics of our Republic? THE PRESENT IS THE EVER MOVING SHADOW THAT DIVIDES YESTERDAY FROM TOMORROW.

IN THAT LIES HOPE.

Frank Lloyd Wright

Taliesin
August 1958

222

APPENDIX

From Ralph Waldo Emerson's Essay on FARMING

THE glory of the farmer is that, in the division of labors, it is his part to create. All trade rests at last on his primitive activity. He stands close to Nature; he obtains from the earth the bread and the meat. The food which was not, he causes to be. The first farmer was the first man, and all historic nobility rests on possession and use of land. Men do not like hard work, but every man has an exceptional respect for tillage, and a feeling that this is the original calling of his race, that he himself is only excused from it by some circumstance which made him delegate it for a time to other hands. If he have not some skill which recommends him to the farmer, some product for which the farmer will give him corn, he must himself return into his due place among the planters. And the profession has in all eyes its ancient charm, as standing nearest to God, the first cause. . . .

Poisoned by town life and town vices, the sufferer resolves: "Well, my children, whom I have injured, shall go back to the land, to be recruited and cured by that which should have been my nursery, and now shall be their hospital." . . .

The farmer times himself to Nature, and acquires that live-long patience which belongs to her. . . .

In the great household of Nature, the farmer stands at the door of the bread-room, and weighs to each his loaf. . . .

The city is always recruited from the country. The men in cities who are the centers of energy, the driving-wheels of trade, politics or practical arts, and the women of beauty and genius, are the children or grandchildren of farmers, and are spending the energies which their fathers' hardy, silent life accumulated in frosty furrows, in poverty, necessity, and darkness.

He is the continuous benefactor. He who digs a well, constructs a stone fountain, plants a grove of trees by the roadside, plants an orchard, builds a durable house, reclaims a swamp, or so much as puts a stone seat by the wayside, makes the land so far lovely and desirable, makes a fortune which he cannot carry away with him, but which is useful to his country long afterwards. The man that works at home helps society at large with somewhat more of

certainty than he who devotes himself to charities. If it be true that, not by votes of political parties but by the eternal laws of political economy, slaves are driven out of a slave State as fast as it is surrounded by free States, then the true abolitionist is the farmer, who, heedless of laws and constitutions, stands all day in the field, investing his labor in the land, and making a product with which no forced labor can compete.

We commonly say that the rich man can speak the truth, can afford honesty, can afford independence of opinion and action—and that is the theory of nobility. But it is the rich man in a true sense, that is to say, not the man of large income and large expenditure, but solely the man whose outlay is less than his income and is steadily kept so. . . .

Who are the farmer's servants? Not the Irish, nor the coolies, but Geology and Chemistry, the quarry of the air, the water of the brook, the lightning of the cloud, the castings of the worm, the plough of the frost. Long before he was born, the sun of ages decomposed the rocks, mellowed his land, soaked it with light and heat, covered it with vegetable film, then with forests, and accumulated the sphagnum whose decays made the peat of his meadow.

Science has shown the great circles in which Nature works; the manner in which marine plants balance the marine animals, as the land plants supply the oxygen which the animals consume, and the animals the carbon which the plants absorb. These activities are incessant. Nature works on a method of *all for each and each for all*. The strain that is made on one point bears on every arch and foundation of the structure. There is a perfect solidarity. . . .

Nature is as subtle as she is strong. . . .

Nature suggests every economical expedient somewhere on a great scale. Set out a pine tree, and it dies in the first year, or lives a poor spindle. But Nature drops a pine-cone in Mariposa, and it lives fifteen centuries, grows three or four hundred feet high, and thirty in diameter—grows in a grove of giants, like a colonnade of Thebes. Ask the tree how it was done. It did not grow on a ridge, but in a basin, where it found deep soil, cold enough and dry enough for the pine; defended itself from the sun by growing in groves, and from the wind by the walls of the mountain. The roots that shot deepest, and the stems of happiest exposure, drew the nourishment from the rest, until the less thrifty perished and manured the soil for the stronger, and the mammoth Sequoias rose to their enormous proportions. The traveler who saw them remembered his orchard at home, where every year, in the destroying wind, his forlorn trees pined like suffering virtue. In September, when the pears hang heaviest and are taking from the sun their gay colors, comes usually a gusty day which shakes the whole garden and throws down the heaviest fruit in bruised heaps. The planter took the hint of the Sequoias, built a high wall, or—better—surrounded the orchard with a nursery of birches and evergreens. Thus he had the mountain basin in miniature; and his pears grew to the size of melons, and the vines beneath them ran an eighth of a mile. But this shelter creates a new climate. The wall that keeps off the strong wind keeps off the cold wind. The high wall reflecting the heat back on the soil gives that acre a quadruple share of sunshine—

> Enclosing in the garden square
> A dead and standing pool of air,

and makes a little Cuba within it, whilst all without is Labrador. . . .

See what the farmer accomplishes by a cart-load of tiles: he alters the climate by letting off water which kept the land cold through constant evaporation, and allows the warm rain to bring down into the roots the temperature of the air and of the surface soil; and he deepens the soil, since the discharge of this standing water allows the roots of his plants to penetrate below the surface to the subsoil, and accelerates the ripening of the crop. . . .

There has been a nightmare bred in England of indigestion and spleen among landlords and loom-lords, namely, the dogma that men breed too fast for the powers of the soil; that men multiply in a geometrical ratio, whilst corn multiplies only in an arithmetical; and hence that, the more prosperous we are, the faster we approach these frightful limits: nay, the plight of every new generation is worse than of the foregoing, because the first comers take up the best lands; the next, the second best; and each succeeding wave of population is driven to poorer, so that the land is ever yielding less returns to enlarging hosts of eaters. Henry Carey of Philadelphia replied: "Not so, Mr. Malthus, but just the opposite of so is the fact."

The first planter, the savage, without helpers, without tools, looking chiefly to safety from his enemy—man or beast—takes poor land. The better lands are loaded with timber, which he cannot clear; they need drainage, which he cannot attempt. . . .

Meantime we cannot enumerate the incidents and agents of the farm without reverting to their influence on the farmer. He carries out this cumulative preparation of means to their last effect. This crust of soil which ages have refined he refines again for the feeding of a civil and instructed people. The great elements with which he deals cannot leave him unaffected, or unconscious of his ministry; but their influence somewhat resembles that which the same Nature has on the child—of subduing and silencing him. We see the farmer with pleasure and respect when we think what powers and utilities are so meekly worn. He knows every secret of labor; he changes the face of the landscape. Put him on a new planet and he would know where to begin; yet there is no arrogance in his bearing, but a perfect gentleness. The farmer stands well on the world. Plain in manners as in dress, he would not shine in palaces; he is absolutely unknown and inadmissible therein; living or dying, he never shall be heard of in them; yet the drawing-room heroes put down beside him would shrivel in his presence; he solid and unexpressive, they expressed to gold-leaf. But he stands well on the world—as Adam did, as an Indian does, or Homer's heroes, Agamemnon or Achilles, do. He is a person whom a poet of any clime— Milton, Firdusi, or Cervantes—would appreciate as being really a piece of the old Nature, comparable to sun and moon, rainbow and flood; because he is, as all natural persons are, representative of Nature as much as these.

That uncorrupted behavior which we admire in animals and in young children belongs to him, to the hunter, the sailor—the man who lives in the presence of Nature. Cities force growth and make men talkative and entertaining, but they make them artificial. What possesses interest for us is the *naturel* of each, his constitutional excellence. This is forever a surprise, engaging and lovely; we cannot be satiated with knowing it, and about it; and it is this which the conversation with Nature cherishes and guards.